AGAINST
the odds

Blacks in the Profession of
Medicine in the United States

AGAINST
the odds

Wilbur H. Watson

Transaction Publishers
New Brunswick (U.S.A.) and London (U.K.)

R
695
.W38
1999

Copyright © 1999 by Transaction Publishers, New Brunswick, New Jersey.

All rights reserved under International and Pan-American Copyright Conventions. No part of this book may be reproduced or transmitted in any form or by any means, electronic or mechanical, including photocopy, recording, or any information storage and retrieval system, without prior permission in writing from the publisher. All inquiries should be addressed to Transaction Publishers, Rutgers—The State University, 35 Berrue Circle, Piscataway, New Jersey 08854-8042.

This book is printed on acid-free paper that meets the American National Standard for Permanence of Paper for Printed Library Materials.

Library of Congress Catalog Number: 98-34953
ISBN: 1-56000-376-6
Printed in the United States of America

Library of Congress Cataloging-in-Publication Data

Watson, Wilbur H.
    Against the odds : Blacks in the profession of medicine in the United States / Wilbur H. Watson.
        p. cm.
    Includes bibliographical references and index.
    ISBN 1-56000-376-6 (alk. paper)
    1. Afro-American physicians—History. 2. Race discrimination—United States—History. I. Title.
R695.W38   1998
610.69'52'08996073—dc21

98-34953
CIP

39545911

Contents

Preface

Although less pronounced since 1954, the forces of racial separatism, gender discrimination, and oppressive dominance have been formidable obstacles against the occupational aspirations of African Americans on the North American continent. Inequalities in access to health care and in the development of professionals in the health services have represented selected effects of these forces.[1] Among the many expressions of these constraints were attempts by some whites to obstruct access by African Americans to medical education and their subsequent practice and mobility within the profession.

Against the background of the history of oppressive dominance in relation to blacks, this study develops insights into successful efforts by a number of determined individuals, small groups of black Americans and philanthropists to establish blacks in the profession of medicine. These streams of successes began with Robert McCune Smith who was awarded the M.D. by the University of Glasgow in 1837. Twenty-seven years later, Rebecca Lee, M.D. (1864), the first black American woman in medicine graduated from the New England Female Medical College.

Then with the end of the Civil War and the founding of the Howard University School of Medicine (1869) and the Meharry Medical College (1876), the educational floodgates were opened.[2] But still, there were numerous challenges to be met. Among them was the need to develop high quality and technologically well equipped hospitals for patient care and specialized training of physicians.

Convincing the public, black and white, that black physicians were competent and creditable providers, no less than their white counterparts has been a more persistent challenge, although waning somewhat in the last half of the twentieth century. These challenges and others have continued to the present day.

Overall, this study develops detailed analyses of (1) social, cultural, political, and psychological factors associated with the practice of medicine by African Americans; (2) race and gender differences in medical education and professional development; (3) first-person reports by older physicians about their personal experiences; (4) doctor-patient relationships during and since the period of racial separatism; and (5) policy implications of physicians' points of view on various issues, such as the vanishing country doctor, folk practitioners as co-participants in health care delivery, ethics, managed care, and the political economy of medical practice in an open society.

Through in-depth interviews and comparative analyses of coping with racial discrimination, segregation, and desegregation, insight is developed into the bearing of separatism on the inner workings of the minds, selves, and social interactions in the professional lives of African American physicians. The analysis is facilitated through conceptual bridges constructed between social, cultural, and demographic factors pertinent to the periods before and after 1954 and the lived experiences of African American physicians in the practice of medicine. Secondly, the text includes excerpts from in-depth interviews of physicians focusing on their techniques of coping with segregation, racial discrimination, and the new challenges brought by desegregation and managed care.

To help assure the reliability of physicians-as-informants focusing on the first half of the twentieth century, I deliberately interviewed two or more who started their medical practices and worked in the same locality for at least ten years before 1954. The assumption was that those physicians who practiced under similar conditions of separatism in the same town or city could cross-validate each other's reports. In the absence of any initial validation, additional data, such as archival records were sought to resolve lacunae and discrepancies. In the absence of any validation, whatsoever, questionable information, such as hearsay, was either excluded from the final descriptors and analyses, or it was simply discussed in endnotes where pertinent. Closing discussions of the book focus on the similar and differing perspectives among black physicians on the humanistic and ethical issues of the day, such as the Tuskegee syphilis experiments (beginning in the 1930s), abortion and the right to life, euthanasia, managed care and the future of African Americans in medicine.

Among the major advantages of this account of the struggles of black physicians are the primary sources on which it builds: older black physicians are engaged by the author through in-depth interviews to tell stories about themselves as physicians and as persons in everyday life.[3] As a consequence, many of the quoted passages in the text are accounts of first-hand experiences and of events of the periods of socially and legally sanctioned racial separatism and the first three decades of de-segregation (1965–1995) in the United States. Because of the primary sources on which the analyses build, especially in parts 1 and 2, this book is unique in the history, ethnography, and social-psychology of blacks in medicine.

In closing, part 3 focuses on developments since desegregation. Special attention is given to demographic change, the decline of country doctors, ethics, the contemporary status of black physicians and recent changes in the social and economic organization of the profession of medicine.

Acknowledgments

The idea for this study grew out of my earlier work on *Black Folk Medicine* (1984). That study raised a variety of questions about the interfaces of folk and modern biomedicine and the development of black physicians in the United States. The latter questions formed the spring-board for the current study.

Formal research was begun in the fall of 1985 through support pro-vided by the United Negro College Fund (UNCF) Distinguished Schol-ars Award. I am grateful to Dr. Luther Stewart Williams, former President of Atlanta University, for nominating me for that award and for his encouragement and support during the early years of the project. The years 1985 through 1987 were focused primarily on field observations and the conduct of in-depth professional history interviews of older black physicians practicing in the black belt of the United States. Dur-ing this period, I also began detailed studies of materials in several archives, especially those of colleges and universities that had devoted resources to the production of black physicians. Through a small travel grant, I was able to spend several weeks studying the archives on black women physicians, then stored at the Medical College of Pennsylva-nia, formerly the Women's Medical College.

This kind of research is rewarding, but extremely time-consuming, expensive, and difficult because of the required travel to small towns and rural settlements "off the beaten track," and the periodic require-ment to take a seat in a doctor's waiting room and patiently await the unscheduled breaks between patients when the doctor would then take time to answer my research-related questions. I am grateful to all of the physicians who took time out of their busy schedules to permit me and my assistants to probe into their professional histories. Ms. Margaret Barnes, Hampton University, assisted in this effort by conducting selected interviews of physicians in the state of Virginia. Similarly, Mrs. Carrie Outlaw, Mississippi Valley State University, assisted in the conduct of selected interviews in the state of Mississippi (see the Appendix on Key Archives and the lists of physicians interviewed).

To facilitate the travel and data collection for this project, I was fortunate to win a second postdoctoral fellowship for the 1988–89 academic year from the William Monroe Trotter Institute of Black Studies of the University of Massachusetts. This fellowship permitted me to spend time in Philadelphia, New York, and Boston focusing in particular on archival materials on women and the social, political, and economic histories of medicine. I am grateful to Dr. Wornie Reed, former director of the William Monroe Trotter Institute and for his encouragement and support of my research during that period.

In recent years Dr. Veronica Scott and the Center on Aging of Meharry Medical College provided support and encouragement, especially related to that part of my research focusing on developments in the state of Tennessee. I am also grateful to Dr. Obie Clayton and the Morehouse Research Institute for staff and technical support, especially in the area of word processing.

One problem with research that occurs over several years and that is national in scope is retaining information about the many people who facilitated the investigation. To everyone I met who cared enough to share his/her thoughts and/or point me in a direction that I might have otherwise neglected, I am grateful.

Because of the special contributions of a few colleagues, they must be singled out. Doris Y. Wilkinson of the University of Kentucky, guided and encouraged me from the beginning when I was trying to decide how best to approach this subject. Irving Louis Horowitz of Rutgers University and Transaction Publishers engaged with me throughout the project in critical dialogue about the conceptual framework and historical scope of the study.

For reading and commenting on selected chapters, I am grateful to Larry Crawford, Ann Baird, and Madison J. Foster of Morehouse College; Ron Manuel of Howard University; the late Nelson Mcghee, Jr. of the Morehouse School of Medicine; Wornie Reed, Cleveland State University; Jennifer Jones Dobbins, University of the District of Columbia and Veronica Scott, Meharry Medical College who carefully read and commented on an early draft of the entire manuscript.

I am also grateful to the anonymous referees selected by Transaction who challenged me to clarify and expand on selected ideas which I previously thought were settled. While I initially found some of their criticisms and questions troubling, after careful reflection and a reexamination of the literature in some instances, rewriting led to important improvements in the manuscript, especially by helping to make it a more comprehensive treatment of the subject.

Between field notes and taped interviews that required transcription, and numerous drafts of each chapter, hundreds of hours of typing and word processing were required for this project. I am grateful to Hattie S. Bell, Pamela Burnett, Priscilla Smalls, Darlita Jones, Jill Spencer, and Tanya D. Young all formerly of Atlanta University, and Motisola Zulu, Kim Devine, Iretha Stoney, and Kanika Bell of Morehouse College for assistance in word processing. Any errors that appear in the writing or composition are my responsibility.

Notes

1. John C. Norman (ed.), *Medicine in the Ghetto* (New York: Appleton-Century Crofts, 1969). See also Wilbur H. Watson, *Black Folk Medicine: The Therapeutic Significance of Faith and Trust* (New Brunswick, NJ: Transaction Publishers, 1984).
2. Charles Victor Roman, *History of Meharry Medical College* (Sunday School Publishing Board, The National Baptist Convention, Inc., 1934; unpublished Master's Thesis, University of Chicago, March, 1945). See also Gary King, "The Supply and Distribution of Black Physicians in the United States, 1900–1970," *Western Journal of Black Studies* vol. 4, no. 1 (Spring 1980), pp. 21–39.
3. For a discussion of the method, see the preface and chapter 8 in Wilbur H. Watson, *The Village: An Oral Historical and Ethnographic Study of A Black Community* (Atlanta, GA: Village Vanguard, 1989).

1

Race, Class, and Power in the Structure of Medical Practice in the United States

Racism, as part of the European white experience, preceded the settlement of the American colonies and became an intricate piece of the colonial period. Racism and segregation were not limited to the South, but were part of the total American experience. Segregation...was a major ingredient in race relations during the 1920s and 30s as access for blacks to the social, political, and economic struc-tures became restricted with time. Segregation was the dominant philosophy which framed black-white relations in the North [as well as the South] and served as the cornerstone for the Supreme Court Case of Plessy v. Ferguson.[1]

This study begins with the assumption that the United States has been a de facto racially stratified and "segmented society" since the inception of the slave trade.[2] Segregated housing, schools, and other race-related structures of everyday life were the principal indicators of segmentation. Dubois (1903) referred to the persistence of inequality and segmentation as "the problem of the color line."[3]

Primary attention in this study is focused on the social and psycho-logical consequences of the "color line" in the practice of medicine among African Americans between 1896 and 1965. However, to facili-tate an understanding of change in African American medical prac-tices, analyses will take into account social structures of race relations and social change in the United States before, during, and since the court approved separatist period framed by the years, 1896 to 1965.

The year 1896 coincided with the *Plessy v. Ferguson* decision usher-ing in a long period of juridical sanctions for "separate" public accom-

1

modations for blacks and whites in the United States.[4] While the U.S. Supreme Court reversed *Plessy v. Ferguson* in 1954 in the case of *Brown v. the Board of Education of Topeka, Kansas*, it was not until the 1965 amendments to the Hill-Burton Act of 1948 that change in federal law struck down the practice of using tax dollars to fund separate hospitals for blacks and whites. Because of the significance of hospitals for the training of surgeons and other specialists in medicine, the primary historical framework of this study was extended beyond the landmark 1954 Supreme Court decision to 1965.

As conceived by Hoetink, a racially segmented social order is characterized by the co-presence in the same society of two or more subgroups that are racially and culturally different from each other with each occupying relatively distinct subregions within the society.[5] This conception is used here for heuristic purposes. There is no presupposition of rigid substantive differences of race or culture between people of African and those of European descent who had settled in the United States by the late nineteenth century. Secondly Hoentik's conception of segmentation does not preclude stratification or social inequalities among the segments. Although major changes have occurred in the United States since the seventeenth century, the slave trade and the forcible use of blacks as chattel laid the foundation for protracted intergroup political and economic inequalities among blacks and whites. It is also clear through careful studies of the substances of legal statutes, juridical decisions, and documented social customs, that there were structural differences in the regulation of the behavior of blacks and whites in everyday life.[6]

There were two broad patterns of racial segmentation observable in the United States during the period between 1896 and 1965: One was indicated by the "black belt" counties and states, (to be defined below) and secondly, by the patterns of racial segregation in housing, public schools, hospitals, clinics, and a variety of other sub-settings in and outside the black belt of the United States. Blacks and whites in the United States are two subgroups of the population whose relationships are, in part, the objects of analysis in this study, especially as those relationships have been expressed in the practice of medicine.

In regard to relations between blacks and whites, my analytic interests are the social, relatively public and private consequences of race-related social oppression, especially the self-imagery of black physicians who completed their medical education and started practices before 1954. Following Goffman,[7] I am concerned about the social construction and management by outsiders (whites) and insiders (blacks) of black identity as a stigma, signifying that "black" stood for something "unusual and bad" about the being of the black physician. To some extent, we will develop social-psychological analyses of the agents provocateurs, white segregationists as it were, whose behaviors, whether deliberately or inadvertently fostered attempts to degrade the professional self-imagery and practices of blacks, but also challenged and motivated many to rise above the vicissitudes of this period in spite of their white counterparts. Chapter 6, on "Race in the Structures of Access to Treatment" and chapter 8, on "Stigma and Coping with Professional Degradation" addresses each of these problems in detail.

The regional starting point is the "black belt" of the United States, defined historically (at least since the U.S. Census of 1790) by the predominantly black counties in the states of Virginia, North and South Carolina, Georgia, Florida, Alabama, Tennessee, Mississippi, Louisiana, and parts of Eastern Texas. By the turn of the twentieth century, the black belt contained an estimated 285 counties of which 55 were at least 75 percent black. But with the decline of cotton, industrialization, out-migration from the South, and other factors, by 1980, the number of counties qualifying by population had declined to 86.[8] The historical density of blacks in these counties was largely determined by the plantation economies, the demand for cheap labor, the use of the slave trade and subsequent generations of their offspring residing in these subsettings and perpetuating the symbiotic relations begun by their parents and other predecessors.

These counties and related states comprised one of the broad subregions of the United States that was still racially segmented (preponderantly black) during the 1970 and 1980 decennial censuses of the United States. Racial segmentation was symbolized by the disproportionately high density of counties that were 51–80 percent black when compared to other subregions of the country. Within the context of the black belt, this study developed insights into the practices of medicine by black physicians, the bearing of race on their practices and their techniques of adaptation to race-related social oppression. Where the data permit, there are also comparisons of experiences of physicians in the black belt and those in other regions of the United States.

Within this broad conceptual framework this study also develops insights into hierarchies of status and class differences within and between members of each segment, blacks and whites, and the bearing of those hierarchies on the profession and practices of medicine among African

American physicians. Of particular interest are indicators of social oppression and the cultural, psychological, and health care consequences for African American physicians, their patients, and families. While attention is focused primarily on the consequences of social oppression and race discrimination in the social structure and organization of the practice of medicine, the affects of gender differences among physicians and patients will also be taken into account. Other factors that influenced the practice of medicine were professional associations, such as the National Medical Association and positions taken by practitioners on ethical issues, such as "the right to life," and physicians' uses of poor, uninformed blacks as subjects in medical experimentation.

It should be noted that the initial plan for this study included intentions to describe and analyze the family lives and religious beliefs of physicians. The assumption was that these factors might help to explain selected features of the personal lives and professional practices of physicians. Unfortunately, the interviews, archival documents and other materials showed that these factors had no significant bearings (or none that were made public) on the professional practices of these physicians. Social oppression, however, was a key concept.

The Concept of Social Oppression

Social oppression is a relational phenomenon expressed through social interaction. In this pattern of interaction, one individual or group deliberately seeks to constrain another to forms of behavior that primarily or exclusively serves the interests of the group that seeks dominance.[9] In practice, this kind of relationship is based upon an unequal distribution of power between the parties involved. As a consequence, the least powerful group, black physicians in this case between the years 1896 and 1965, were subject to the risk of being oppressed in the performance of various courses of action, such as attempting to admit patients to hospitals to facilitate their medical care. In spite of their demonstrated competence in medicine and achievements in the profession, African American physicians often suffered social, professional, and psychological degradation. There were widespread beliefs that blacks were inferior to whites and should in no way be treated as their equals in either professional or social relations. The following passage is illustrative:

One day the telephone rang.... "Doc, I want to have a favor from you. My wife is at Doctor's Hospital. Dr. Hernandez [a white physician] is going to do a hysterectomy on her. Will you go and assist him?" I said, "but I taught you. You assisted me in two or three hysterectomies. You want my frank opinion?" "Yea," [said the caller]. I said, "you go to hell." I regret it. I was at the Port of Christ. You see, I practiced medicine at Port of Christ. But, I didn't go. Now here is a black doctor...for whom you have performed miracles. But, his wife who had to have a hysterectomy has to have a white man. Black physician! Now, the facts are there. If you tell me Christianity is a reason for it, I challenge you to that. It's not easy to be a Christian. I lost my cool. I didn't go out and get fresh air, but I told him to go to hell. But, right now we're both very good friends. I encouraged him to go to medical school and so forth, but there is something about blacks that we haven't found yet. What it is, I don't know.[10]

This quotation illustrates one of the leveling effects of race-related social oppression. In spite of his academic and professional achievements, this practitioner complained that he was rejected, in this instance, as a creditable surgeon because of the color of his skin. Ironically this act of rejection, albeit symbolic, was expressed by one of his own black medical colleagues.[11] Here, as Fanon previously observed, a contemporary agent of oppression need not be identical racially to members of the historical oppressor group.[12] Once conditioned to believe and act as if one's racial or ethnic group is culturally and professionally inferior, a previously colonized people or members of any other oppressed group, such as African Americans, can be induced to act against their own self-interests and those of their kindred by aiding and abetting their historical oppressor. This outcome is referred to by Memmi[13] and Freire[14] as a consequence of the internalization of the oppressor.

To the extent that one individual or group expresses subservience to another through observable social behavior, it is reasonable to assume that either, or a combination of the following, events has occurred or is in the process of becoming a completed act: (1) The subservient party in the relationship will have either been forced into that position or will have become oppressed by default through political apathy and complacency; or (2) The oppressed individual or group will have internalized the demand characteristics of the oppressor by making them his or her own.[15] Under these circumstances, albeit inadvertent, the oppressor and the object of oppression may enter a complementary relationship. In intergroup relations, however, where members of one group, such as seventeenth-century Africans, became the objects of control by another, such as slave traders, there may be degrees of unevenness in the extent to which the members of the group targeted for control will express compliance with or show willful subservience in response to the party that seeks dominance.

In this study of African American physicians, the dominant group during the period between 1896 and 1965 was comprised of white segregationist members of the medical profession and their lay (non-medical) counterparts in American society-at-large. The research will develop insight into: (1) the social and cultural consequences of patterns of dominance by whites in relation to blacks; (2) indicators of the internalization of the oppressor by some black physicians and patients; (3) the associated discriminatory treatment, segregation, and stigmatization of blacks by whites and blacks on the basis of race; and (4) the bearing of various patterns of dominance and segregation on the self-perceptions of black medical doctors and their practices.

Status Relations and Society in the Southern United States

While some literature fosters the impression that racial separatism had its most profound expression in institutions of the southern United States, we will show that some black physicians in northern regions of the country were not spared the affects of the color line.[16] It is interesting to note in this regard that some idealists among black physicians in the South turned their eyes northward after reaching the threshold of their tolerance for frustrated attempts at achieving peaceful coexistence and congenial collaboration in medical practices with whites in the South. The background to one Louisiana physician's decision to leave the South for a new start in New Jersey, a northeastern state, illustrates this dilemma:

> I was fortunate in that I inherited the practice of a physician who had an unfortunate incident to happen to him. He had gone to Mississippi to a conference and coming back here [to New Orleans], he was arrested in some small town because he stopped by the road to eat his lunch and after he ate, he "watered" [urinated] in a canteen, then poured it out on the side of his car. They arrested him for indecent behavior. He was very popular. His wife was from Boston. So, they brought him before the magistrate, and he told him, "your honor, I didn't do anything wrong. I'm a doctor." The judge said, "I don't give a God-damn who you are." He said, "to me, you're just another nigger." So he [the black physician] came back here [to New Orleans] and packed his bag and told me, he said, "you can have it. I'm going to New Jersey." And he moved. It's been about thirty years and he's been there ever since.[17]

During the first half of the twentieth century, segregation in race relations and oppressive dominance of blacks, in particular, was widespread, easily noticeable, and much more taken for granted in the South than in other regions of the United States. Yet, racial segregation, patterns of dominance, and discrimination were not peculiar to the South. Although more subtle in some instances, racism was a significant factor also in the organization of health care, even in states as far north as Massachusetts where it was believed by some observers that blacks enjoyed the greatest degree of social equality.[18] Before taking a close look at the incentives for northward migration of black physicians and reported experiences associated with their northern medical practices, it will be useful to frame this discussion in the broader context of postbellum racial differences, North and South, in the social structure of occupations and professions.

Class, Status, and Medical Practices in the North

From the close of the Civil War up through World War I, there were few black Americans in the northern United States when compared to the South.[19] There were few if any "Negro Jobs," such as servants, nor vested interests in black laborers by a "white master class" as there had been in the pre-Civil War South.[20] In other words, there was no protection of selected jobs or "race roles" for blacks.

While status relations between Southern blacks and whites were widespread and culturally sanctioned before the Civil War, with continuing expressions of these kinds of relations well into the twentieth century, the relations between blacks and whites in the North were more impersonal and based on class. Northerners tended to adhere to rules of equal treatment in extrafamilial and other impersonal relations such as in voting rights, but exercised greater selectivity in filling positions that could lead to personal relations, such as with servants and nannies where intimacies were more likely to develop. While there were widespread sentiments in the northern United States that blacks should be given the franchise to vote and the right to full citizenship under the laws of the land, there were also competing sentiments that "the Negro ought to stay where he belongs on the Southern farm land."[21] These sentiments that symbolized the idea of a place set aside for blacks and tolerated by whites helped to form the bases of widespread practices of segregation and discrimination in housing, occupations, and professions; restricted access to institutions for education, hospitals, and many other public accommodations. Similar sentiments were found in the thinking of the American Colonization Society, founded early in the nineteenth century and dedicated to founding a separate society for freed slaves somewhere outside the United States.[22] It was also these white-supremacist values and beliefs that helped to frame the contents of professional practices in medicine between 1896 and 1965.

To reiterate a point made earlier, it is understood that neither race relations before 1896 nor since 1965 have been fully free of the structural constraints described above. That is not an issue here. The period between 1896 and 1965 was chosen as a point of departure for theoretical and methodological reasons: To facilitate inquiry into the behavioral consequences of socially and legally sanctioned racial separatism in the practice of medicine by blacks during the late nineteenth and early twentieth-century United States.

Looked at from the point of view of findings about the experiences of African American professionals and small black-owned businesses in the city of Detroit before 1896, some black physicians in the northern United States were sharply restricted in opportunities for medical practices as were some black physicians in the South. While higher education and the acquisition of skills favorable to the practice of medicine helped to open windows of opportunity for some, the "color line" sharply limited opportunities for mobility and success for the majority of black physicians even in the North.[23] For example, while Dr. Samuel C. Watson came to Detroit in 1863 and lived there for more than twenty years, he was prohibited from practicing medicine in Detroit.[24] Other vocations, however, such as politics and livery services were open to him as they were to other blacks.

> In 1863 [Samuel C. Watson], established one of the most successful prescription drugstores in the city and quickly rose to the forefront in black political activity. Born in South Carolina in 1832, Watson had been orphaned at age nine and became the ward of a Washington, DC Presbyterian minister. An 1857 graduate of Western Homopathic College, at Cleveland Medical School, Watson had previously attended Phillips Academy in Andover, Massachusetts, Oberlin College, and the Medical School of the University of Michigan. He had practiced medicine in Chatman, Ontario upon graduation from medical school and in Toronto from 1861 to 1863. In between [he] had followed the path of gold fever across Canada to the gold fields of British Columbia. His forte, however, was business and politics and he met with immediate success in Detroit. A leading Detroit citizen, the heavy-set, light-skinned, mutton-chopped Watson served on both the Board of Estimate and the Common Council of Detroit, and in 1884 served as a delegate to the Republican National Convention; the first Negro Delegate from the North.[25]

Regardless of the kind of business undertaken by northern blacks, the major products and foci of black businesses after the Civil War were the delivery of goods and services to white clients. This pattern extended from the early postbellum period through the 1940s.[26] The masses of African American consumers in the north simply were less resourceful, economically, than their white counterparts and were less able to purchase the services of the developing black entrepreneurs. Moreover, this race- and class-related pattern in the consumption of goods and services of black businesses held as well for consumers of physicians' services.

The majority of fee-for-service patients of practicing black physicians in the north were white during the early years of blacks in medicine.[27] It was not until after World War II that the black community in Detroit, for example, was sufficiently large and financially strong to become major consumers and supporters of a substantial number of black businesses and professions.[28] The significance of this observation on the economics of support for blacks in medicine is made more poignant by Myrdal in his perspective on the economic resources of blacks by the mid-twentieth century:[29] "The poverty of the Negro people limits the opportunity for Negro businessmen and professionals. Since they are excluded from the white market, it becomes important for them to hold the Negro market as a monopoly...."

While this quote from Myrdal draws attention to the relations among race, business and professional opportunities during the 1940s, by the mid-1960s, no significant change had occurred in the relationships among these factors.[30] The prevalence of relatively low median individual and family incomes still limited the ability of black consumers to support only a few black proprietors of businesses and professions.[31]

It is true that African American entrepreneurs have experienced some improvements since World War II as results of growth in the black "middle class," diversification in business development, and their abilities to attract new clients, black and white. Nevertheless, black entrepreneurs still depend largely on black consumers for support and tend to locate their businesses in black neighborhoods.[32] Chapter 7, on "Doctor Shopping Behavior" and chapter 12 on the "Contemporary Status of Black Physicians" raises this point into bold relief. The analyses show that race prejudice is still widespread, expressed through discrimination by black and white patients and in referrals by some white and selected black physicians. Where black physicians are concerned, some prospective patients, white and black, especially, but not exclusively in the South did not turn to black doctors for health care because of race prejudice and skepticism about the abilities of black physicians to competently practice medicine. Yet blacks have been the majority of the patients of black physicians throughout their presence in the profession of medicine. This distribution, however, may change with the progress of desegregation and the growth of managed-care organizations.

Conclusions

This chapter sets forth the basic assumptions and broad conceptual framework of this study. It is assumed that the United States has been, historically, a racially stratified and divided society. Except for the period between 1896 and 1965, that division was primarily a consequence of social custom, not law. While taking into account, broadly, how race relations helped to shape the development of medicine in the United States, the special focus is on black physicians who completed their medical education and began to practice medicine between 1896 and 1965. This period was selected, analytically, to facilitate initial inquiry into the differences that legally and socially sanctioned racial separatism might have made in African American practices of medicine, and to facilitate systematic inquiry.

The stigmatization of black physicians and the social-psychological consequences, thereof, is a special focus. By stigma is meant an attribute of individual or group character that is believed to signify something unusual or bad about the being of the signifier. For example, in the history of white American social thought, people of African descent, popularly identified by dark complexions, were erroneously believed to be culturally depraved and mentally inferior when compared to their white counterparts. Being stigmatized because of the color of their skin was a concern to many black physicians especially as that stigma affected their professional practices. This is a theme that is recurrent throughout the chapters of this book.

Intentional social oppression is a second key concept that helps both to explain the social construction and uses of stigmatization and, subsequently, the diminished self-imagery of individuals and groups that tends to develop therefrom. While some white physicians interviewed for this study denied individual intentions to oppress their black counterparts in the profession of medicine, claiming instead their capitulation to local social custom that produced those outcomes, by willful compliance with those customs, they nevertheless contributed to the oppression of blacks. The problem and social-psychological consequences of oppression will also be recurrent themes throughout these chapters.

Finally, the African American physician faced multifaceted struggles, whether (1) in southern or northern regions of the country; or (2) in coping publicly (in hospitals, clinics or medical school faculties); or (3) privately with the constraining and degrading effects of race-related separatism. In some instances, as this study will show, some of the greatest challenges came from other African American physicians and patients. In other cases, the struggles included tests of personal fortitude, the extent to which the individual black physician was personally determined to succeed in spite of the broadly based separatist social customs and professional opposition that he or she faced. More recently, since 1965, the major challenges have come through the political and economic effects of desegregation and managed care, organizational changes that have undermined the previous justifications for black only hospitals and the consignment to black physicians, albeit by default, of black patients.

These, then, are the central themes: (1) the problem of stigmatization on the basis of race prejudice; (2) the social construction and rationalization of oppressive dominance; (3) desegregation, the development of managed care, and the simultaneous unraveling of black hospitals and the structural protection of black patients for black physicians that resulted from segregation; finally, there was (4) the determination to succeed in the profession of medicine by many African American physicians in spite of these obstacles. Each part of this book and the chapters therein build upon the broad conceptual framework set forth in this introductory chapter. While any given part can be studied separately from the whole, the broadest possible perspective and deepest understanding will be achieved through a careful reading of the text in its entirety. With this understanding, let us proceed to part 1 on "The Struggles to Achieve Medical Education and High Quality Health Care for African Americans."

Notes

1. Ira C. Colby, "The Freedmen's Bureau: From Social Welfare to Segregation," *Phylon* vol. 46, no. 3 (Sept. 1985), p. 228.
2. This assumption is based upon my reading of race relations in the history of the United States. See, for example, John Hope Franklin and Alfred A. Moss, *From Slavery to Freedom* , 7th ed. (New York: McGraw-Hill, 1994), pp. 429–432. See also John Hope Franklin, *Race and History: Selected Essays, 1938–1988* (Baton Rouge, LA: Louisiana State University Press, 1989). For the working concept of racially segmented societies, see H. Hoentik, *Caribbean Race Relations: A Study of Two Variants,* translated from the Dutch by Eva M. Hooykaas (New

York: Oxford University Press, 1967). The concept of segmentation is not to suggest rigidity. For a discussion of variations in degrees of segmentation among key states, see A. Leon Higginbotham, Jr., *In the Matter of Color: Race and the American Legal Process, The Colonial Period* (New York: Oxford University Press, 1978).

3. W.E.B. Dubois, *Souls of Black Folk* (New York: Fawcett Publications, 1961).
4. Rayford W. Logan, *The Betrayal of The Negro: From Rutherford B. Hayes to Woodrow Wilson.* (London: Collier Books, 1965); see also Allison Davis, Burleigh B. Gardner, and Mary R. Gardner, *Deep South: A Social Anthropological Study of Caste and Class* (Chicago: University of Chicago Press, 1965), p. 337.
5. Hoentik, *Caribbean Race Relations.*
6. Logan, *The Betrayal of the Negro*; see also Higginbotham, *In the Matter of Color,* and John Hope Franklin, *The Color Line* (Columbia, MO: University of Missouri Press, 1994).
7. Erving Goffman, *Stigma: Notes on the Management of Spoiled Identity* (Englewood Cliffs, NJ: Prentice-Hall, 1963).
8. Anne S. Lee, "The Elderly in Black Belt Counties," in Wilbur H. Watson (ed.), *The Health of Older Blacks: Social and Demographic Factors* (Atlanta, GA: Center on Health and Aging University, 1987).
9. Frantz Fanon, *Black Skin, White Masks* (New York: Grove Press, 1967), p. 10; See also Paulo Freire, *Pedagogy of the Oppressed* (New York: Herder and Herder, 1970). For another point of view, see Philip Mason, *Patterns of Dominance* (New York: Oxford University Press, 1970).
10. Jean Breire (M.D.), professional history interview, Shreveport, Louisiana, February, 1986, pp. 28–29. For a general perspective on race relations in the first half of the twentieth century, see Gunnar Myrdal, *The American Dilemma* (New Brunswick, NJ: Transaction Publishers, 1996).
11. Not only did this physician complain that he was not asked to perform the hysterectomy on the wife of this black colleague whom he had also taught , he also complained because the same colleague asked him to assist a white surgeon whom he preferred to treat his wife.
12. Fanon, *Black Skin.*
13. Albert Memmi, *The Colonizer and the Colonized* (Boston, MA: Beacon Press, 1967).
14. Friere, *Pedagogy of the Oppressed.*
15. Ibid. Also see Fanon, *Black Skin.*
16. E.H. Beardsley, "Making Separate Equal: Black Physicians and the Problems of Medical Segregation in the Pre-World War II South," *Bulletin of the History of Medicine* vol. 57 (Fall 1983): 382–96.
17. George Thomas (M.D.), professional history interview, New Orleans, Louisiana, August 1986, pp. 9–10.
18. Arnold M. Rose, *The Negro in America,* with a foreword by Gunnar Myrdal (Boston: Beacon Press, 1948), p. 103.
19. Franklin and Moss, *From Slavery to Freedom,* pp. 343–344.
20. Rudolph Morias, *African American Physicians* (New York: Basic, 1978), p. 30.
21. Rose, *The Negro in America,* p. 142.
22. Charles S. Johnson, *Bitter Canaan* (New Brunswick, NJ: Transaction Publishers, 1987).
23. Rose, *The Negro in America,* p. 101.
24. David M. Katzman, *Before the Ghetto: Black Detroit in the Nineteenth Century* Urbana, Illinois: University of Illinois Press, 1973, p. 127–128.
25. Ibid., p.127.

26. Ibid. Also see Rose, *The Negro in America*, p. 128.
27. Katzman, *Before the Ghetto*.
28. Ibid., p. 130.
29. Myrdal, *The American Dilemma,* p. 108.
30. See Allison Davis, Burleigh B. Gardner and Mary B. Gardner, *Deep South*: *A Social Anthropological Study of Caste and Class* (Chicago: Phoenix, 1965).
31. E. H. Beardsley, "Dedicated Servant or Errant Professional: The Southern Negro Physician before World War II," pp. 142–167 in *The Southern Enigma*: *Essays on Race, Class and Folk Culture*, ed. Walter Fraser, Jr. and Winfred B. Moore, Jr., (Westport, CT: Greenwood Press, 1983); and Alphonso Pinkney, *The Myth of Black Progress* (New York: Cambridge University Press, 1984); see also Wilbur H. Watson, *The Village*: *An Oral Historical and Ethnographic Study of a Black Community* (Atlanta: Village Vanguard, Inc., 1989), pp. 106–123.
32. Bart Landry, *The New Black Middle Class* (Berkeley and Los Angeles, CA: University of California Press, 1987), pp. 43–57; see also John Sibley Butler, *Entrepreneurship and Self- Help among Black Americans: A Reconsideration of Race and Economics* (Albany, NY: State University of New York Press, 1991); St. Clair Drake and Horace Cayton, *Black Metropolis* (Chicago: University of Chicago Press, 1987); and E. Franklin Frazier, "Durham: Capitol of the Black Middle Class," pp. 333–340 in Alain Locke (ed.), *The New Negro* (New York: Athenaeum, 1968).

Part 1

The Struggle to Achieve Medical Education and High Quality Health Care for African Americans

Introduction to Part 1

The development of African Americans in medicine in the United States has been a long and convoluted journey. From the graduation of the first black medical doctor (Glasgow, 1837) to the dawn of the twenty-first century, the challenges for blacks who sought membership and practice in the profession of medicine have been arduous, often discouraging, but not without many outstanding efforts by various individuals, small professional associations, philanthropists, and selected medical schools that withstood the adversarial conditions and achieved some measures of success.

With respect to blacks and women in the United States, there have been two major social historical forces functioning to constrain (or limit to small numbers) their access to the ranks of medical practitioners: *racism* and *sexism*. Nevertheless, there have been several modest but positive developments that will be discussed in chapters 2–12 against the background of the following social historical periods: (1) the pre-Civil War period to 1861; (2) the post-Civil War period (1868) to *Plessy v. Ferguson* (1896); (3) the period of legal separatism in medical practices in the United States, 1896 to 1965; and (4) the post-separatist or desegregation period, 1966 to the dawn of the twenty-first century.

The development of the topics in chapters 2–4 and 9–12 will correspond, but not adhere strictly in sequence to these historical periods. Each chapter contributes to an understanding overall of the broad political, economic, and professional challenges faced by African American physicians in the long journey from the pre-Civil War dawn of their access to biomedical education to the current post-separatist period of desegregation.

The special focus and contribution of chapter 2 is on medical education. The state of Tennessee is given special attention because of the development of six different programs of medical education for blacks in that state between 1876 and 1900. Partly because of its major influence on state legislative decision making and the closing of several black medical schools, the Flexner Report of 1910 is also given special attention in chapter 2.

Chapter 3 is devoted to "Gender in the Development and Practice of Medicine." While women of color suffered some of the same outcomes of race discrimination as their male counterparts, there were differences between them as a consequence of gender. Race and sex are closely linked with status differentiation and inequalities in the history of occupations, professions and career development in the United States. The bearing of race and male dominance, especially sexist beliefs and values on gender roles, has been especially important in the career aspirations and achievements of African American women in medicine. Gender discrimination intruded through rules fostered by males against sexually integrated student bodies in medical schools, deliberate goading of women to select certain specialties, such as pediatrics and obstetrics-gynecology (ob-gyn), and other degradation ceremonies.

The ownership and/or control of hospitals were significant factors in the technological development of medicine, improvement of the quality of care of patients and, in particular, the development of surgical specialties. Surgery, more than any other specialty required the aseptic environment and selected technological resources that were best provided by hospitals. It was not coincidental that the prestige and high financial return of surgeons was closely associated with, and tightly controlled by, white male physicians. As such, attempts by blacks to develop and operate their own hospitals took on economic and political significance: in order to cultivate this specialty during the period of racial separatism, black physicians had to become aggressive in the development of hospital facilities less they be constrained, except in small numbers, from ever cultivating the skills and becoming competitive in this prized sub-area of the profession. Chapter 4 is devoted to a detailed discussion of hospital development and management in relation to blacks in medicine. Other insights into the social organization of hospitals are developed in chapters 6, 7, 9, and 12.

2

History and Political Economy of African American Medical Education

> *In their haste to become Americans, their desire not to be peculiar or segregated in mind or body, they try to escape their cultural heritage and the body of experience which they themselves have built-up. This is the reason that there is always a certain risk in taking a colored student from his native environment and transplanting him suddenly to a northern school. He may adjust himself. He may through the help of his own social group in the neighborhood of this school successfully achieve an education through the facilities offered. On the other hand, he may meet peculiar frustration and in the end be unable to achieve success in the new environment or fit into the old. For these and analogous reasons, I am convinced that there is a place and a continuing function for the small Negro college.*
> —Dubois (1946)[1]

This chapter develops an analysis of the political and economic contexts of the medical education of black physicians in the United States. Highlighted are the developments of the Meharry Medical College and the Howard University School of Medicine, the Flexner report of 1910 and its influences on selected programs for medical education of blacks, and the obstacles faced by blacks in achieving residencies for specialized training.

Special attention is focused on six different initiatives to develop programs for African American medical education in the state of Tennessee between 1876 and 1900. The Meharry Medical College is the best known and the only one of these institutions that survived, grew stronger, and continues today. Far more interesting, however, is the

19

fact that Tennessee was the setting for these six institutions while, in some black belt states, like Mississippi, Georgia, and Alabama that had significantly larger African American populations, there were no concerted public or private movements for medical education of blacks. Moreover, among the other states where there was active work toward the development of institutions for the medical education of blacks, no state other than Tennessee spawned more than one institution. More detail on these observations will be discussed later in this chapter.

The graduation of David John Peck (1847) from Benjamin Rush Medical School marked the dawn of black achievements in medical education in the United States. Although small in number and scattered around the country, the next twelve years following Peck's success witnessed the efforts of several other African American individuals and established institutions of higher education to pave the way for an increasing presence of blacks in medicine.

At least five colleges or schools of medicine admitted and/or conferred M.D. degrees upon one or more African Americans during the period from 1848 to 1860. It should be noted, albeit not to diminish the achievements of these African Americans, that this was a historical period when national academic requirements for the M.D. degree required only two years attendance at prescribed lectures with a school year lasting 5–6 months. Included among these pioneering institutions and individuals were the following:

- Bowdin College of Maine. Conferred the M.D. degree upon John V. de Grassa, 1849.[2]
- Harvard Medical College. Admitted Martin R. Delaney, Daniel Laing, and Issac H. Snowden, 1850. Because of student and faculty protests against "race mixing," these students were expelled early in the spring of 1851 (see chapter 3 for details).[3]
- Dartmouth College. Conferred the M.D. degree upon Daniel Laing, 1854[4] (Laing was one of the three African American students expelled from Harvard in 1851).
- Western Homeopathic College of Cleveland, Ohio. Conferred the M.D. degree upon Samuel C. Watson, 1857.[5]
- New England Female Medical College. Admitted Rebecca Lee, 1860 first African American woman in medicine in the United States, and conferred the M.D. degree upon her in 1864.[6]

These antebellum successes are noteworthy, considering the entrenched institutions of slavery in the Southern United States and the associated patterns of oppression and discrimination against blacks that were current during that period of American history. It is also noteworthy that, with the exception of Cleveland, Ohio, all of the institutions that conferred M.D. degrees on blacks between 1848 and 1864 were in the New England states, well outside the domain of the slave South. Significant educational opportunities for large numbers of African Americans, however, did not begin until after the Civil War.

> For blacks, equal rights, higher education, and recognition in the white society were out of the question until a glimmer of hope appeared with the signing of the Emancipation Proclamation in 1863 releasing blacks from slavery. Unfortunately, the glimmer quickly dimmed for the black woman who still had to break down the more subtle barriers of...sex.[7]

The Need for African American Medical Education

The exclusion of African Americans from medical education and practice in the context of a steadily increasing population of blacks in

FIGURE 2.1

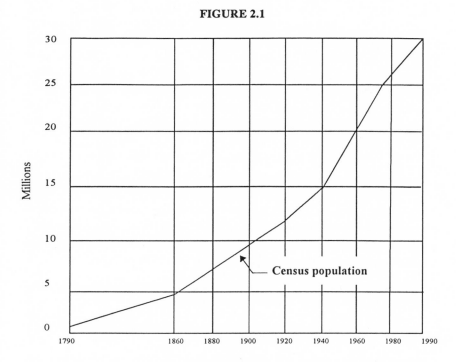

Resident Black census population for selected years: 1790–1975. Facts of Life and Death. No. PHS. 79-1222. National Center for Health Statistics. Washington, DC: Government Printing Office, 1978. The 1990 data were selected from Claudette E. Bennett, Current Population Reports, Population Characteristics, p. 20–464. *The Black Population in the United States.* March, 1991, p. 133, table 3. Washington DC: U.S. Department of Commerce, Economics and Statistics Administration, Bureau of the Census, March, 1991.

the United States (along with the separatist practices of white physicians) helped to stimulate the need for more black physicians. As shown in figure 2.1, the population of African Americans in the United States has grown steadily since the first census in 1790.

While there was growth in the production of black physicians, beginning with the small trickle initiated by James McCune Smith in 1839 (Glasgow), by the year 1970, African Americans were still significantly underrepresented among the ranks of physicians in the United States. For example, although blacks comprised 11 percent of the total population in 1970, only 2 percent of the physicians in the United States were black.[8] This percentage, by the way, represented significant growth that had occurred since the Supreme Court ruling on *Brown v. Board of Education of Topeka, Kansas* (1954) and the passage of the Civil Rights Acts of 1963 and 1964. While 83 percent of all black physicians in the United States had been trained through Meharry Medical College and the Howard University School of Medicine through the early 1960s and 1970 half of the first-year students in Medical Schools since the Supreme Court decision were matriculated at predominantly white universities.[9] Nevertheless, improvements are still needed. By the year 1990 blacks were still underrepresented in the profession (3.2 percent) relative to their percentage of the general population, 12.3 percent of the United States.[10] As chapter 3 will show, women were even more underrepresented than black men among physicians.

The First Century of Black Medical Education in the United States, 1847–1947

In spite of the health care needs of African Americans, and the interests of many in pursuing degrees in medicine to help meet those needs, access to predominantly white medical schools before the Civil War and during the reconstruction period was almost nonexistent.

> In the South and border states where the vast majority of Negroes lived, they were denied admission to white schools. Few were qualified and financially able to apply to the northern schools in the first place and a major segment, with a rudimentary secondary education was ill prepared to matriculate at either Howard or Meharry.[11]

Nevertheless, the strong desire for medical education did not subside. Pressures were exerted to open medical schools where blacks could be admitted without the discriminatory treatment that was so widespread in existing schools. Partly in response to this need, eight additional programs of education for blacks developed between 1880 and

1900 contributing to the production of new physicians begun by Howard and Meharry within the decade after the Civil War. Nevertheless, with the development of new standards for medical education that became mandatory following the Flexner Report of 1910, each of these post-1880 initiatives had closed by 1923. In the discussion presented in a later section of this chapter on "failed attempts in other states to establish medical education for blacks," the focus and findings of the Flexner Report are described. In addition to the Howard University School of Medicine and Meharry Medical College, we will also describe the eight new programs of medical education for African Americans that developed in the United States between 1880 and 1900. First, however, descriptions of the programs of Howard University and Meharry Medical College are set forth.

Howard University

Howard University opened its doors on 20 November 1866, named in honor of Major General Oliver Otis O. Howard, administrator of the War Department in Washington, DC. Under General Howard's orders, construction of the "Freedmen's Hospital and Asylum" also began on the grounds of Howard University at Fifth and W Streets, Northwest, Washington, DC.

The Howard University School of Medicine was incorporated 2 March 1867. Its doors were formally opened 9 November 1869. The Howard School was primarily intended to train "colored doctors," but was officially open to all, regardless of race, color, or creed. A part of the distinction of the Howard School and its development after the Civil War was the fact that "there was no previous record of Negroes attending medical school below the Mason-Dixon line in the antebellum period" and only a small number attended schools in the North. [12]

Other features that distinguished the Howard University School of Medicine in the early years were as follows:

1. Low tuition. (Kept low for the benefit of poor students. Many had to work their way through.)
2. Inclusion of women in the student body. Unlike the white medical schools, women students were welcomed in recognition of the kinship of blacks and women in the equal rights movement. [13]
3. During the long depression of 1873, tuition was rescinded and not reinstated for seven years (1880), and then it was kept very low. [14]

At its inception, the Howard University School of Medicine had five faculty members, four of whom were white. Dr. Alexander T. Augusta was the sole Negro.[15]

Meharry

The Meharry Medical College was founded in 1876 as the Medical Department of Central Tennessee College in Nashville, Tennessee.[16] The Medical College was intended "solely for the education of black doctors to look after the urgent health needs of the masses of their race in the South. It was a de jure racial institution."[17] Five white men, the Meharry brothers, provided the money for a four- story brick structure that became the permanent home of Meharry. One source gives the following account of the inspiration for the interest and contributions of the Meharry Brothers.

> In some of the rough experiences of their boyhood pioneering days, the Meharry Brothers were helped by one or more individuals of the colored race. Their gratitude survived, and in the mature years of prosperity took a practical missionary form. They responded to local appeals for funds to establish a Medical College for colored people, and furnished the money to purchase the site for the college that bears their name. [18]

After thirty-nine years of operation and receiving commendations from the Flexner Report, the State of Tennessee granted the school a new charter on 13 October 1915, that "provided for its separate corporate existence without university affiliation."[19] This arrangement has continued until this day.

Meharry was privately financed. Unlike Howard, Meharry received no government support in the early years. Its first faculty, Dr. Hubbard and Dr. Snead (a Confederate army surgeon) were white.[20] Meharry achieved recognition from the American Medical Association in 1923 under its new president, Dr. John H. Mullowney (a white physician). At that time, it was rated a "grade-A institution," a distinction it has held ever since.[21] Today, Meharry like Howard, has discarded its commitment to a segregated student body, and now opens its doors to all.[22]

The Ascent of African American Medical Education in Tennessee

By the end of the nineteenth century, there was a growing demand for high quality education with clear distinctions between secondary school, college, and university levels. Included among these were public demands for improvement in quality standards of medical education in the United States. Out of these concerns there developed a study of 155 American and Canadian medical schools undertaken between 1908 and 1910 by Abraham Flexner on behalf of the Carnegie Foundation.[23] It should be noted that the broad mandate of the investigation for the Carnegie Foundation was to seek insight and recommend means of improving academic and professional training programs in general, public and private, not merely medical education.

Secondly, Flexner's study was not focused upon African American medical education, but upon medical education in general. His findings showed that there had developed a weakening of emphasis on high quality as a result of: (1) an over-emphasis among medical schools on the commercialization of medical education and practice, especially but not exclusively, during the twenty-five years before his study; (2) a lack of close public and private scrutiny and monitoring of standards in medical education; and (3) a relative absence in the minds of the public of any discrimination between well trained and poorly trained physicians.[24] Merely appending the label M.D., which was all too easily done as a mark of identity, was widely accepted as symbolic of competence to practice medicine.

As noted earlier among the ten programs of medical education established between 1869 and 1900 to increase the production of African American medical doctors, only the Meharry and the Howard University programs survived the post-Flexner period. While the Flexner Report was not the sole cause of the demise of the other programs of medical education, in the case of five of them, Flexner's findings did have considerable influence on subsequent actions by the Rockefeller General Education Foundation and state legislative assemblies in selecting those medical schools to which financial support would be given.[25] The Rockefeller General Education Foundation, for example, gave approximately $100,000,000 to those schools which Flexner recommended for support, of which only Howard and Meharry were included from among the ten with a special mission to train African American physicians.[26] In the following discussion, we will describe those schools for the Medical Education of African Americans that got low marks in the Flexner Report and closed their doors by or before the year 1923.

To begin this discussion, let us return first to the state of Tennessee wherein there were five other attempts (in addition to Meharry) to establish programs of medical education for blacks each beginning, like Meharry and Howard, between the end of the Civil War and the turn of the century. Unlike Meharry, each of the other five programs in Tennessee had short periods of survival.

The Knoxville College Medical Department 1895–1900[27]

Prior to the Civil War there were no medical schools for African Americans anywhere in the United States. The earliest documented effort in this regard was undertaken in 1862 by the United Presbyterian Church of Nashville, Tennessee.[28] This institution was founded "for the purpose of befriending the friendless, homeless Negroes who flocked into Nashville."[29] While it is not clear that this institution actually began medical education for blacks in 1862, that is the impression given in *Medical Men & Institutions, 1789–1957.*[30]

The Nashville program for medical education, originally established by the Presbyterian Church for general education of Negroes, was moved to Knoxville in 1875. By 1890, the school had been considerably upgraded to organize and offer college classes.

During the period between 1887 and 1900, the Presbyterian church offered the buildings and grounds of its educational facility to the University of Tennessee. Those facilities and the educational program became the "'Colored Department' of the University of Tennessee."[31] Subsequently the "Colored Department" of the University of Tennessee became the Medical Department of Knoxville College in 1895. The Department was sustained for only five years and was discontinued in 1900. Included among its African American faculty were William Wallace Derrick, M.D., an 1892 graduate of the Meharry Medical Department, Central Tennessee College, Nashville. After graduation from Meharry, Derrick went directly to Knoxville to set up a practice and was subsequently appointed professor of chemistry and physical diagnosis at the Knoxville College Medical Department in 1896.

Knoxville Medical College, 1900–1910

The Knoxville Medical College was the third and least successful of the three medical colleges for blacks that was visited by Flexner in January, 1909 during his study of *Medical Education in the United States and Canada.*[32] This particular institution was organized in the City of Knoxville late in the year 1900 following the demise of the Medical Department of Knoxville College that was affiliated with the University of Tennessee as its "Colored Department," 1895–1900.[33]

The Knoxville Medical College was an independent institution when visited by Flexner. Its entrance requirements were nominal, a high-school diploma or less was required for admission. There were twenty-three students enrolled, with eleven staff persons, nine of whom were professors. Dr. Blanche Beatrice Thompson, a 1901 graduate of Meharry Medical College and one of three African American women physicians in the city, was an instructor in phrenology at the College. It is interesting to note that Dr. Thompson was one of her husband's instructors who was himself studying at the time for a degree in medicine from Knoxville Medical College.[34]

The Knoxville Medical College occupied a floor above an undertaker's establishment with neither laboratory nor clinical facilities, including the absence of a dispensary.[35] In regard to clinical education, a student informed Flexner that twice during each academic year, a few students were taken to the Knoxville College Hospital; that was the extent of clinical education.[36] In May 1902, the College graduated two students.[37] These conditions, no doubt, helped to account for the closing of the school in 1910.

Three other little known attempts at the development of institutions in the state of Tennessee for the medical education of blacks should be mentioned. These programs are described below in order by the date of their founding, from the earliest, 1889 to the latest, 1899. Each rose and fell before the Flexner study, and perhaps for that reason, are not acknowledged in Flexner's 1910 publication.

The Hannibal Medical College 1889–1896 (Memphis)[38]

This institution was incorporated and opened its doors in October, 1889. According to McHollin and Hamburg,[39] this college was founded by a Dr. Cottrell, graduate of a Department for training black physicians in Arkansas. The faculty of Hannibal Medical College, comprised of five professors, was racially mixed: two white and three black. According to one source, Hannibal produced five graduates.[40] It became extinct in 1896, thirteen years before the Flexner study.

Medical Department of the University of West Tennessee (Memphis), 1900–1923

The Medical Department of the University of West Tennessee was founded in 1900 by Dr. Myles V. Lynk, a black physician. The Department developed in two phases. First it was organized at Jackson, Tennessee in 1900 where it remained for seven years. Then in 1907, its facilities were moved to Memphis.[41] During the twenty-three years of its existence, this Department graduated between 216 and 266 students of whom 98 (37 percent) passed the State medical boards.[42]

In addition to founding this Department of Medicine, Dr. Lynk published the first black medical journal in the United States, *The Medical and Surgical Observer*.[43] This publication appeared successively for eighteen months and a total of seventeen issues.

At the time of Flexner's site visit in November 1909, there were forty students in attendance, with fourteen teaching staff, all of whom were professors. There was no record of the racial composition of the faculty. Students were admitted with a high-school education, the standard for most colleges of the period. Laboratory facilities were meager, barely equipped for work in chemistry, pharmacy, and microscopy. Facilities for clinical education were also poor: students had access to eight or ten beds, twice weekly, in a small nearby hospital. Flexner concluded that this Medical Department was without merit and should be closed.[44] And so it was in 1923.

Chattanooga (Tennessee) National Medical College 1899–1908

This college had a short lived existence that also ended before the Flexner study began. Therefore, while its demise may have occurred because of the kinds of inadequacies found by Flexner in other colleges, it has not been demonstrated that this college was a victim of the Flexner Report.

According to one account, this college never got started as a producer of graduates. Although it had nearly a ten-year existence, there was no record of any graduates except the years 1901 and 1902.[45] No details were found that accounted for the demise of this college.

Four Theoretical Notes on the High Density of Institutions for Medical Education of Blacks in Tennessee

Antebellum Prevalence of "Herrenvolk Democratic" Beliefs

As noted in the opening discussion of this chapter, Tennessee was distinguished from other states in the United States during the late nineteenth century by the number of institutions developed to foster medical education of African Americans. While the evidence is not conclusive, my analysis suggested that the following factors were favorable to these outcomes: there were broadly based *"herrenvolk* democratic" beliefs, values and rules of long standing pertaining to the rights of freedmen, white Tennesseans, and the northern Union forces that occupied Tennessee following the Civil War. (The idea of *herrenvolk* democracy will be discussed in detail below). Secondly, there were widespread sentiments among white Tennesseans that education was a right of African Americans. Moreover, it was believed that education was a major means of developing civilization and cultivating manners of deportment among blacks favorable to making them a people acceptable to their white counterparts. While these sentiments may have portrayed paternalistic and white supremacist frames of references, they were nevertheless favorable in the state of Tennessee to the influx of sizable sums of public and private money in support of higher education for African Americans during the 1880s.[46] Now, let us examine the idea of *herrenvolk* democracy.

Herrenvolk democracy refers to a biracial society in which one racial group oppresses and tyrannizes another. By denying that the subordinate race is fully human, the oppressor group rationalizes its dominance and its claim to a "democratic ideology" for its own members.[47] This conception, it will be noted, is consistent with Hoentik's idea of a racially stratified and segmented society as formulated in chapter 1.[48]

While not acknowledging African Americans as fully human, many conservative white Tennessee paternalists and some northern white "liberals" from the 1880s through the mid-twentieth century felt responsibility for the uplift of blacks.

> To most whites, the past enslavement of blacks and their lack of education, property, and political experience rationalized the need for a policy of white paternalistic guidance..."we must go forward with the experiment of Negro civilization, education, and elevation." Since whites bore the responsibility for the Negroes' presence in the South, common fairness, to say nothing of our superiority and the demands of morality and religion, requires that we shall care for their education and elevation to a plane of intelligence and conscience that will make them safe and useful citizens.[49]

Although this quotation does not explicitly show white Tennessean support for medical education of blacks, it does show a foundation of beliefs and values present in the 1880s favorable to statewide investments in programs of education, such as the programs of the medical schools documented in this chapter. It should be noted that, with the exception of the Meharry Medical College, founded in 1876, and the Hannibal Medical College, founded in Memphis in 1889, the other four medical schools in Tennessee were founded between 1895 and 1900. The significance of this observation is that sentiments in support of liberal education for African Americans had begun to wane toward the end of the decade of the 1880s, perhaps not coincidentally, as the doctrine of separatism was becoming increasingly popular throughout the United States.

Political Economy of Tennessee and Sentiments against the Confederacy and Slavery

Tennessee was a border state standing between deep South confederate and northern interest groups at the dawn of the Civil War. On the matter of secession, its citizenry were divided. The majority, however, were in favor of the state remaining in the union so long as it was not required to furnish troops to either side.[50] While the sentiments in favor of remaining in the union were not restricted to any sector or subgroup within the state, they were stronger in the eastern sector that included Knoxville.[51] Several factors helped to account for the pro-union and/or anti-slavery (if not neutral) sentiments on slavery in eastern Tennessee.

Because of the mountainous terrain in eastern Tennessee, farms were small. As a consequence, there were neither the financial means nor demand for cheap farm labor, such as slaves, in contrast to owners of large cotton, tobacco, and other plantations of the Deep South. Similarly, slaves could not be profitably used on small southern farms nor for that matter in factories of the northern states.[52]

The state's distinction as the only member of the Confederacy to abolish slavery by its own act in February, 1865 was a second factor suggesting statewide sentiments favorable to improvements in the quality of lives of African Americans in Tennessee. Two other indicators of a bond, and shared values with the Union was the state's resistance to leaving the union to join the Confederacy, the last state to do so in 1861, and the first to be readmitted to the union in 1866.[53]

Lincoln's 1864 nomination for a second term to the presidency of the United States and the Republicans search for a "Southern Union Man" for the vice presidency led to the choice of Andrew Johnson, then governor of Tennessee, to be Lincoln's running mate. It was probably not coincidental that with the end of the Civil War, the assassination of Lincoln and Johnson's succession to the presidency (April 1865), that the headquarters of the newly formed and organized Freedmen's Bureau was located in Nashville, Tennessee.[54] Through sentiments varying from neutrality on the question of secession in western Tennessee to modest support for the union in eastern Tennessee, plus the rise of a favorite son to the presidency and the power of the Freedmen's Bureau based in Nashville, the social and political conditions were established favoring the elevation of African Americans in that state.

Major General Oliver Otis Howard (for whom Howard University was named) was appointed head of the Freedmen's Bureau. Howard and his assistants took the position that the former slaves must be put in positions to help themselves and that one of the most urgent "wants" of the freed people was education.[55]

The presence of the Freedmen's Bureau was felt throughout the state. The Bureau took the position that former slaves should have equitable access to public education and health care to enable the eradication of disease and facilitate substantial improvements in the overall quality of their lives. Members of the Freedmen's Bureau thought that education was the key to combating the poverty and misery of the newly freed slaves.[56]

Meharry, A Beacon of Hope

The founding of Meharry Medical College in Nashville in 1876 was another key factor that helped to foster broad support for African American medical education in Tennessee. By its presence and successful graduation of three physicians in 1878, Meharry and these new medical doctors became role models; beacons of hope for other African Americans who aspired to the craft of medicine. It was graduates of Meharry, such as Miles V. Lynk (class of 1891), who in several instances lead the way in founding the new Departments of Medicine in West Tennessee, Knoxville, and Chattanooga and in providing the faculty needed by each. As pointed out earlier, Miles V. Lynk was founder of the "Medical School of West Tennessee," established in Jackson, Tennessee in 1900. After its doors closed in 1907, Lynk moved the program to Memphis to form the College of Medicine of the University of West Tennessee.

The Imperative of Avoiding Race Mixing

"As long as racial mixing was in no way involved, most whites in

Tennessee favored the education of Negroes at public expense."[57] For whites, the fear of gradually eroding all "barriers of race" was the problem that many began to believe might develop through education and other extensions of liberties to blacks. Miscegenation, in particular, was most opprobrious to whites. For example, a part of the rationale for the Knoxville Medical Department, that was funded by the state through the University of Tennessee was based on a recognition that blacks needed physicians, but must not be permitted to attend classes side by side with whites at the University of Tennessee Medical School.

In sum, the unusually large number of programs of medical education for blacks in Tennessee were not merely results of general public sentiments favoring medical education for blacks. Instead, the following hunch seems plausible: the support shown in the state was in part deliberately conceived by some white philanthropists (inside and outside the state), state legislators, and others out of an attempt to help blacks meet their own needs for health care and by doing so, mitigate or forestall attempts by blacks to gain admission to the sacred halls of white medical schools, such as the Universities of Nashville and Tennessee. This idea is consistent with Stanfield's analysis of selected attitudes of "progressive white liberals" toward blacks between the late 1920s and the 1940s in the United States.[58] Stanfield suggested that the belief among whites that they should take initiatives on behalf of blacks was not due merely to their charitable dispositions. Instead, many whites felt threatened by the urbanizing black population and thought that the encroachment of blacks into white neighborhoods, schools, and other institutions could be forestalled if blacks were given resources or helped to cultivate the means to develop their own effective leadership and institutions.[59]

Another set of factors that raise questions about the intentions of white philanthropists and public sources of support is the observation that the level of financial and technical support given most of the medical schools for blacks was meager and quantitatively less valuable than the private support given, for example, to Meharry. This conclusion is suggested by the fact that none of the other five programs of medical education in Tennessee survived the post-Flexner period of medical education. It will be recalled that three of these programs met their demise even before the publication of the Flexner report. Assuming the reasonableness of these hypotheses, further study should show that blacks must have represented little or no threat to whites in other Southern states, such as Georgia, Alabama, and Mississippi where, in spite of their large numbers and health problems, there were no documented efforts in those states toward developing institutions for African American medical education during the post-Civil War period. It is probably true also that sentiments in favor of education for blacks were not as widespread in the other states of the black belt.

Short-Lived Programs of Medical Education in Other States

Leonard Medical School of Shaw University
(Raleigh, North Carolina), 1880–1915

At Martha's Vineyard, Massachusetts, 1880, the Trustees of Shaw University voted to establish a medical school. The school started with a small Medical Dormitory in the fall of 1880, large enough to house six students. By 1881 with the erection of the Leonard Medical Building, the school was expanded to an enrollment of fifteen students. The erection of the Leonard Medical Building was made possible through "generous donations from 'northern friends,' especially Godson W. Leonard of Hampden, Massachusetts and other members of his family."[61]

The land on which the Medical school was founded was contributed to the City of Raleigh by the North Carolina legislature. The construction plan was to include a medical building, hospital, dispensary, and a dormitory. The hospital, however, was not erected until 1885.[62] In addition to substantial state aid, the school was supported by the Baptist Missionary Society for Negroes.[63]

While the Leonard School was intended to train African American physicians, at its inception, two of its three faculty were white. By the time of the Flexner study in 1909, there was a teaching staff of nine, eight or whom were professors.[64]

It was noted earlier that the Leonard Medical School was one of ten educational institutions developed in the South for the purposes of training African American physicians during the post-Civil War period (see the appendix of this chapter for the full list of other schools). The first graduating class of the Leonard School numbered only 6 in 1886. By 1909, however, when Flexner visited the institution there were 125 students in attendance. By 1915, over 500 students had earned the M.D. degree through this institution.[65] One of these graduates was John A. Kenney, who later became distinguished as Booker T. Washington's family physician, as medical director of the John A. Andrew Hospital of the Tuskegee Institute, and as one of the founding members of the National Medical Association. Nevertheless the Leonard School did not receive high marks in the Flexner Report.

According to Flexner:

> This [The Leonard School] is a philanthropic enterprise that has been operating for well-nigh thirty years and has nothing in the way of plant to show for it. There are no library, no museum, and no teaching accessories. Clinical facilities are hardly more than nominal. The school had access to a sixteen-bed hospital, containing at the time of the visit in [1909] three patients. [The Leonard School] cannot, except at great expense maintain clinical teaching. The way to help the Negro is to help the two medical schools that have a chance to become efficient, Howard at Washington, Meharry at Nashville.[66]

Upon closing the Leonard School in 1915, its total number of graduates had risen to 574.[67] Unlike Tennessee and the District of Columbia, the political, economic, and cultural conditions in Kentucky, Louisiana, and North Carolina were less favorable to sustained growth of black medical schools or colleges and the prevention of their demise following the Flexner report. Our attention is now turned to the states of Kentucky and Louisiana.

Louisville (Kentucky) National Medical College 1881–1911

The Louisville National Medical College was founded by Dr. Henry Fitzbutler, 1888, for training of African American physicians.[68] Fitzbutler was previously distinguished as the first African American to practice medicine in the state of Kentucky, 1871–1901.

The Louisville National medical college was opened with the sanction of the Kentucky State legislature in 1889. Like many of the medical schools of the pre-Flexner period (before 1910), the Louisville National Medical College admitted applicants with less than a high school education. By the time of the Flexner study in 1909, attendance at Louisville had grown to forty students, with a staff of twenty faculty, seventeen of whom were professors.[69] Like the other schools that were downgraded by the Flexner Report, the Louisville National Medical College was unable to withstand the post-Flexner criticism and gain political and economic support to perpetuate its existence. It did succeed, however, in graduating twenty-nine students before its closing in 1911.[70]

New Orleans(Louisiana) University Department of Medicine,
1889–1910

New Orleans University was founded by the Freedmen's Aid Society, 1869, for the education of Negroes in Louisiana. It was originally named Union Normal (1869) and, was renamed New Orleans University in 1872.[71]

In 1889, New Orleans University added a Department of Medical Education that was renamed the Flint Medical College in 1910 in honor of John D. Flint, a philanthropist who had made generous donations to support the college.[72] Between 1889 and 1901, the Department of Medicine, subject to considerable criticism because of low enrollment, started with only ten students and inadequate funds to support medical education. The absence of clinical teaching facilities, such as an affiliated hospital, and meager laboratory equipment diminished the quality of the educational program throughout its existence. Not until 1896, seven years after the founding of the Department of Medicine at New Orleans University, was the Phyllis Wheatley Sanitarium officially opened, a thirty-bed hospital facility, that provided a means of clinical training of Negro physicians enrolled at the Flint Medical College.[73]

Even though improvements were made in funding and teaching facilities between 1889 and the turn of the century, they were not sufficient to meet the criticisms and challenges of the Flexner report. By the time of the Flexner study in 1909, flint had an enrollment of twenty-four students, and a teaching staff of fifteen, of whom six were professors, all practitioners.[74] The laboratory facilities were poorly equipped for training and experiments in anatomy, chemistry, pathology, and bacteriology. By 1909, Flint still controlled a twenty-bed hospital (ten beds fewer than those opened by the Phyllis Wheatley Sanitarium in 1896) with an average daily attendance of one or two patients.[75] Nevertheless the Flexner Report concluded that "Flint Medical College is a hopeless affair, on which money and energy alike are wasted."[76] The Flint Medical College closed its doors in 1910, after which the building of the college and the Sarah Goodridge Hospital were merged to form a single physical plant, a fifty-bed hospital, called the "Flint-Goodridge Hospital."

While gaining access to medical school was an important first step toward establishing a career in the profession of medicine, securing a residency to establish a specialty was much more difficult for blacks during the period of racial separatism. Not the least of the difficulties for African American men and women were the racially discriminatory treatments of them by white gatekeepers of predominantly white medical centers. These centers were the best equipped to provide the widest range of training for a specialty, particularly, but not exclusively in surgery.

Specialist Wanted, No Blacks Need Apply: The Elusive Residency

Residency is the opportunity to study under a preceptor in a specialized area of inquiry and practice through which the recent graduate of a medical school seeks to establish credentials for him or herself. Surgery, cardiology, obstetrics and gynecology, pediatrics, and oncology are just a few of the medical specialties for which residencies are sought by young medical doctors. In addition to developing competency in a specialty, a residency helps to prepare the young physician for state boards which, if passed, provides the license for practice in a specialty. For a variety of reasons, of which racial discrimination was preponderant, few black physicians succeeded in achieving residencies in the United States between 1896 and 1965.

> When I came out [of military service, 1944], it was hard for a black to find a residency anywhere. I had been in the Army for four years and had been separated from medicine. While I practiced some in the Army, I was more of a first aid man, what you call more of a sanitation officer than really a doctor. When I came out, I looked for a place [for a residency]. I went all over the East and West, Chicago, New York, Philadelphia and those places.[77]

In spite of exclusion from major white hospitals and universities, many young African American physicians of this period were innovative in finding ways of developing their competencies in specialized areas.

> Just a sparse few could go to a white hospital, or somewhere and get an internship. And then to get residency training, this you just didn't know about. Nobody thought about getting residency training. The thing that appealed to me and most of the folks who were interested was that, if you went to a small hospital and worked there for a couple of years, you could learn the fundamentals of treating people.[78]

Specialties wherein Blacks Gained a Foothold

As a consequence of discrimination against African American men and women who sought residencies, many became general practitioners, known today as family physicians. Among African American physicians, there was little demand for the skills of specialists, other than ob-gyn, pediatrics, and medical missionaries. Even among those, however, who developed specialties in ob-gyn or pediatrics, developing a successful practice was not assured:

> Well, the thing about it is they thought that we weren't trained as well as whites. In spite of that belief, I imagine I was the only pediatrician at one time here [Durham, North Carolina] who had a post-doctoral degree, you know, in pediatrics. But, that didn't make any difference. you would be surprised how ignorant some of the [white] professors were at the college, complaining about the training that black physicians had.[79]

Rural versus urban settings for medical practices were also important factors in the determination of success. For example, in regard to probable financial return on investments to establish private practices, there was little incentive in terms of patient demand for services for African American physicians to develop practices in small towns and rural areas of the country.

Comparisons of areas of specialization of black men and women physicians before 1965 showed similar distributions in the types and rank orders of specialization in each group: Ob-gyn, pediatrics, tropical medicine, psychiatry and general medicine. The more technical specialties, such as pathology, ophthalmology, physical medicine and rehabilitation, and surgery did not begin to show up in substantial numbers among the ranks of African American physicians until after the supreme court decision of 1954 (*Brown v. Board of Education of Topeka, Kansas*) and the amended Hill-Burton Act of 1965.

In the more prestigious specialties, such as surgery, blacks had their greatest difficulty in getting access to residencies and becoming board certified. As told by an older African American physician:

> It is true that whites in many parts of the country tried to prevent blacks from becoming surgeons. It's protection for their [whites'] positions; that's number one. Number two would be the adequacy of training of blacks to become surgeons, which was minimal. Where could you get training? In little [black] hospitals, they [black physicians] learned how to take out an appendix, or a tonsil,... In [white] hospitals where black [doctors] couldn't go to take a patient for a medical ailment,... you know they couldn't go for a surgical problem. This is what existed then.[80]

In another case, an African American physician of fair complexion who wanted a residency in surgery had his application accepted by the white establishment, but was later fired when his actual racial identity was uncovered.

> The doctor of note had finished the University of Michigan in 1933. He got an internship at the receiving hospital in Detroit and I guess they assumed he was white cause he was coming from Michigan with that name. He was fired the day he arrived cause he was black. He went on and did a residency at Homer. G. Phillips, as you know was originally St. Louis Hospital Number Two [and later became Homer G. Phillips]. He became a surgeon and practiced in Detroit for a long time.[81]

Conclusions

This chapter described and analyzed selected features of the history of medical education for African Americans. Special attention was focused on the ten medical departments and/or schools developed in the late nineteenth century to train African American physicians in the United States. The Morehouse School of Medicine and the Drew Post-Graduate Medical School are late twentieth century developments, which are discussed in more detail in chapter 12.

Up through the Civil War in the United States, there was but a trickle of blacks entering and graduating from medical schools. Then with the end of the war and the founding of the Howard University School of Medicine and the Meharry Medical College, the production of black physicians showed a steady increase.

A surprising finding was the presence of six different institutions for the medical education of blacks in the state of Tennessee. Each had its inception between 1876 and 1900. The most distinguished and only survivor of that period was the Meharry Medical College. Four theoretical excursions are developed to offer potential explanations for these unusual events in the state of Tennessee.

In closing, attention is turned to obstacles faced by black medical doctors in gaining access to residencies. Rather than crumble under the oppressive weight of racism, periodic powerlessness, segregation, and economic depravity, many African Americans chose to struggle against these odds to uplift themselves. Along with the efforts by black men and women and some generous philanthropists to open the doors to medical education, there were many successful attempts to develop and operate their own hospitals (a topic that is discussed in detail in chapter 4). There were also a small number, but relatively successful efforts to form health and life insurance companies and other kinds of intervention and self-help programs. Because of the special circumstances related to sexism and racial discrimination in the development of careers in medicine, the next chapter is devoted to that topic.

Notes

1. W.E.B. Dubois, "The Future and Function of the Private Negro College," *The Crisis,* vol. 53 (Aug. 1946), pp. 234–46, 253–54. See alsoW.E.B. DuBois, *The Education of Black People: Ten Critiques, 1906–1960,* ed. Herbert Aptheker (Amherst, MA: University of Massachusetts Press, 1973) pp. 139–148.
2. W. Montaague Cobb, "James McCune Smith: First Black American M.D." *Journal of the National Medical Association,* vol. 73 (suppl. 1981), p. 1205; see also Werner Sollors, Thomas A. Underwood, and Caldwell Titcomb (eds.), *Varieties of Black Experience* (Cambridge, MA: Harvard University Department of Afro-American Studies, 1986), p. 28.
3. Sollors et al., pp. 21–28; see also W. Montague Cobb, "Delany the Redoubtable" and "Holmes and Harvard," *Journal of the National Medical Association,*" vol. 73 (suppl. 1981), pp. 1205–1208.
4. Sollors et al., p. 27.
5. David M. Katzman, *Before the Ghetto: Black Detroit in the Nineteenth Century* (Urbana, IL: University of Illinois Press, 1973), p. 127.
6. Archive on Black Women Physicians, file K-Z, Medical College of Pennslyvania, August 1988.
7. "Early Black Women Physicians," *Women and Health,* vol. 5, no. 3 (Fall 1980), p. 1.
8. James L. Curtis, *Blacks, Medical Schools, and Society* (Ann Arbor, MI: University of Michigan Press, 1971), p. vii.
9. Ibid., pp. xi–xii.
10. These percentages are drawn from the National Data Book, *Statistical Abstract of the United States, 1992* (Washington, DC: U.S. Department of Commerce, Economics, and Statistics Administration, Bureau of the Census, 1992), pp. 17 and 392.
11. Aubre de 1. Maynard, *A Gallery of Negro Surgeons* (vol. 1, unpublished and undated), The Amistad Research Center, New Orleans, Louisiana, 23–21 November 1985, p. 108. [It should be noted that the Amistad Research Center, formerly located in the Old U.S. Mint at 400 Esplanade in the back of the French Quarter was moved to Tulane University in the fall of 1986].
12. Ibid., vol. 1., p. 95.
13. Ibid., vol. 1., p. 99.
14. Ibid.
15. Ibid., pp. 97–98.
16. Ibid., p. 102.
17. Ibid., pp. 98, 246.
18. For more detail, see Charles V. Roman, *Meharry Medical College: A History* (Nashville, TN: Sunday School Publishing Board of the National Baptist Convention, 1934, Appendix A, p. 199, see archives, Meharry Medical College Learning Resources Center archives].
19. Maynard, *A Gallery,* p. 102; Also see Charles V. Roman, *Meharry Medical College: A History.*
20. Ibid., p. 103.
21. Ibid., pp. 104–105.

22. Ibid., pp. 105.
23. Abraham Flexner, *Medical Education in the United States and Canada: A Report to the Carnegie Foundation for the Advancement of Teaching* (New York: The Heritage Press, 1973), pp. vii–x.
24. James Riley Montgomery, " The Volunteer State Forges Its University: The University of Tennessee, 1887–1919," *The University of Tennessee Record,* vol. 69, no. 6 (Nov. 1966), pp. 131–145. It is worthy of note that this document shows detailed discussions about the importance of founding a core medical school among faculty and administrators of Vanderbilt University, the University of Tennessee, and the University of Nashville at the turn of the century, but no reference is made to Meharry Medical College, although it was clearly operational in Nashville at that time.
25. Flexner, *Medical Education*, pp. 181, 202–203, 233 and 307–309.
26. Ibid., pp. 108–181.
27. Maynard, p. 109.
28. Samuel Joseph Platt and Mary Louise Ogden, *Medical Men and Institutions of Knox County Tennessee*, 1789–1957 (Knoxville, TN: J.B. Newman Printing Company, 1969; see archives, the McClung Collection, Lawson McGhee Library, Knoxville, Tennessee].
29. Phillip M. Hamer, *The Centennial History of the Tennessee State Medical Association*, 1830–1930 (Nashville, TN: Tennessee State Medical Association, 1930), p. 405. Although some authors, such as Mattie McHollin and Cheryl Hamburg distinguish the Jackson and Memphis programs as two different schools, in my analysis, these programs and locations are regarded as one combined initiative that occurred in two phases to establish a program of medical education in western Tennessee. See Mattie McHollin and Cheryl Hamburg, "Black Medical Education in Tennessee," Fall Meeting of Tennessee Archivists, 15 Nov. 1991, p. 5, archives, Meharry Medical College.
30. Platt and Ogden, *Medical Men and Institutions*.
31. Ibid.
32. Ibid., pp. 303–304.
33. Hamer, *The Centennial History*, p. 104.
34. There was no record of any other graduates. Also serving among African Americans on the faculty beginning in 1902 at the Knoxville Medical College was Henry Morgan Green, M.D., who earned his degree in medicine from Knoxville Medical College in 1901. He was a professor of bacteriology, histology, pathology and anatomy. Dr. Edwards L. Watkins, also a graduate of the college returned to join the faculty in 1909 as professor of obstetrics and gynecology. For more detail see Platt and Ogden, *Medical Men and Institutions*.
35. Platt and Ogden, *Medical Men and Institutions*.
36. Flexner, *Medical Education in the United States.*
37. Platt and Ogden, *Medical Men and Institutions*, p. 75.
38. Hamer, *The Centennial History*, p. 403.
39. McHollin and Hamburg, "Black Medical Education in Tennessee."
40. Ibid.
41. Hamer, *The Centennial History*, p. 405.
42. Maynard, *A Gallery*, p. 108. See also Hamer, *The Centennial History*, p. 405. There is a wide gulf between the number of graduates reported by these two sources; 266 by Maynard and 216 by Hamer.
43. Maynard, *A Gallery.*
44. Flexner, *Medical Education*, pp. 305, 309.
45. Hamer, *The Centennial History*, p. 404.

46. Joseph H. Cartwright, *The Triumph of Jim Crow*: *Tennessee Race Relations in the 1880s* (Knoxville, TN: The University of Tennessee Press, 1976), pp. 177–182.
47. Ibid., pp. 164–165. See also Pierre L. Van den Berghe, *Race and Racism*: *A Comparative Perspective* (New York: John Wiley and Sons, 1967), pp. 17–18.
48. H. Hoentik, *Carribean Race Relations*: *A Study of Two Variants,* translated from the Dutch by Eva M. Hooykaas (New York: Oxford University Press, 1971).
49. Cartwright, *The Triumph of Jim Crow*, p. 178.
50. J.E. Overall, *The Study of Tennessee* (Dansville, NY: F.A. Owen Publishing Company, 1961; see archives, Knoxville College Library, Knoxville, TN).
51. Ibid., p. 29.
52. Ibid.
53. Ibid. It is ironic that while Tennessee lead the way in programs of medical education for blacks, needed to foster health care and protect them from disease, the state also spawned the first organized activity of the Ku Klux Klan, 1866, in Pulaski, Tennessee. For further insight, see Overall, *The Study of Tennessee*, p. 33.
54. James Summerville, *Educating Black Doctors*: *A History of Meharry Medical College* (Tuscaloosa, AL: The University of Alabama Press, 1983), p. 3. The Freedmen's Bureau was created by an Act of Congress in 1865 as the "Bureau of Refugees, Freedmen and Abandoned Lands." It was placed in the War Department and given authority over all subjects relating to refugees and freedmen in the former rebel states.
55. Ibid.
56. McHollin and Hamburg, "Black Medical Education in Tennessee."
57. Summerville, *Educating Black Doctors*, p. 178.
58. John Stanfield, "Epilouge," pp. 227–34 in Charles S. Johnson, *Bitter Canaan*: *The Story of the Negro Republic* (New Brunswick, NJ: Transaction Publishers, 1987).
59. Ibid., p. 234.
60. Wilmoth A. Carter, *Shaw's Universe*: *A Monument to Educational Innovation* (Rockville, MD: D.C. National Publishing, Inc., 1973), p. 30.
61. Ibid.
62. Ibid., pp. 31, 223.
63. Ibid., p. 107.
64. Flexner, *Medical Education*. There was no breakdown of the racial composition of the faculty in 1909.
65. Ibid.
66. Ibid., pp. 281–282.
67. Ibid.
68. Maynard, *Gallery,* vol. 2, p. 307. Also see Flexner, *Medical Education*, p. 230.
69. Flexner, *Medical Education*
70. Maynard, *Gallery*
71. John Duffy, *The Rudolph Matas History of Medicine in Louisiana* (Louisiana State University Press, vol. 2, 1962), p. 548.
72. Ibid.
73. Ibid., p. 526.
74. Flexner, *Medical Education,* p. 275.
75. Ibid.
76. Ibid., p. 233.
77. George Thomas (M.D.), professional history interview, New Orleans, LA, 1986, p. 7.

78. Leroy Upperman (M.D.), professional history interview, Durham, NC, 2 May 1986, p. 5.
79. William A. Cleland, (M.D.), professional history interview, Durham, NC, 1986, p. 11.
80. Upperman, pp. 6–7.
81. Watts (M.D.), professional history interview, Durham, NC, 1986, pp. 22–23.

Appendix

Chronology of African American Medical Schools*

	Founded/Closed
Howard University School of Medicine Washington, DC	1869–ongoing[a]
Meharry Medical College Nashville, Tennessee	1876–ongoing[b]
Leonard Medical College (A division of Shaw University) Raleigh, North Carolina	1880–1915[c]
Louisville National Medical College Louisville, Kentucky	1888–1911[a]
New Orleans University Department of Medicine (renamed the Flint Medical College, 1901) New Orleans, Louisiana	1889–1910[d]
The Hannibal Medical College Memphis, Tennessee	1889–1896[e]
Chattanooga National Medical College Chattanooga, Tennessee	1899–1908[e]
Medical Department of The University of West Tennessee Memphis, Tennessee	1900–1923[f]
The Knoxville College Medical Department, Knoxville, Tennessee	1895–1900[e]
Knoxville Medical College Knoxville, Tennessee	1900–1910[e]

Twentieth Century Developments of African-American Medical Schools

The Drew Post Graduate Medical School Los Angeles, California	1968–ongoing
The Morehouse School of Medicine Atlanta, Georgia	1978–ongoing

[a]Flexner, Abraham, *Medical Education in the United States and Canada: A Report to the Carnegie Foundation* (New York: The Heritage Press, 1973); see also Aubre de L. Maynard, *A Gallery of Negro Surgeons,* vol. 1 (n.p, n.d., The Amistad Research Center, New Orleans, Louisiana, 1985), p. 367.

[b]Summerville, James, *Educating Black Doctors: A History of Meharry Medical College* (Tuscaloosa, AL: The University of Alabama Press, 1983).

[c]Carter, Wilmonth A., *Shaw's Universe* (Rockville, MD: D.C. National Publishing. Inc., 1973), pp. 30, 223–224.

[d]Duffy, John (ed.), *The Rudolph Matas History of Medicine in Louisiana*, vol. 2. (Baton Rouge, LA: Louisiana State University Press, 1962); see also Flexner, *Medical Education*.

[e]Hamer, Phillip M., *The Centennial History of the Tennessee State Medical Association*, 1830–1930 (Nashville, TN: Tennessee State Medical Association, 1930), p. 404; see also Phillip M. Hamer, *Tennessee: A History, 1673–1932* (New York: The American Historical Society, Inc., 1933), p. 957.

[f]Miles v. Lynk, *Journal of the National Medical Association,* vol. 44, no. 6 (Nov. 1952), p. 475.

3

Gender in the Development and Practice of Medicine by Blacks

The woman who today enters a profession appears to be doing a casual thing. The fear of a woman unsexing herself was the bugbear of that period (1870). Only level headed, determined, self-reliant women then ventured to take a step likely to elicit unfriendly criticism; likely to induce disparagement, if not estrangement.

—Brown (1923)[1]

Being female in this last bastion of male dominance and imagined supremacy may be the overriding source of stress and conflict for most black women who became surgeons. The male physician, and in particular the male surgeon, is loath to admit that surgery is, after all, a very feminine endeavor. Surgeons nurture, care for, and empathize with the ill. Cutting and sewing with delicacy and grace in the operating room is merely an extension of what women have been doing in the home for centuries. It is the man who has to learn at age twenty-five or thirty what his female colleague has been doing since the age of five or six.

—Sterling (1987)[2]

Research on gender in the development and expression of medical practices among blacks is scarce.[3] When gender is combined with a focus on the constraints of racial separatism, especially between 1896 and 1965, even fewer studies are reported in the literature.

Gaining access to training in the profession of medicine was one of the persisting difficulties faced by blacks who aspired to become medical doctors in the United States. In addition to the well-known effects of racial separatism on institutions of public and private education,[4] gender differences also had important influences on access to services and professional development. Women, for example, who sought higher education had to struggle against the protagonists of both sexism and racism.[5]

Among the predominately white northern medical schools, the New England Female Medical College, the University of Chicago, and the Medical College of Pennsylvania (formerly the Women's Medical College) were leaders among the institutions admitting blacks, men and women, during this period. Nevertheless, the majority of black medical doctors were graduated by the Meharry Medical College in Tennessee and the School of Medicine at Howard University in Washington, DC.

The First Black American in White

James McCune Smith (1811–1865) was the first black American man to receive the M.D. degree; this event occurred in 1837.[6] Smith's degree, however, was not earned in the United States. Although he finished the New African Free School in New York, and was the son of a prosperous and influential merchant in New York City, Smith was unsuccessful in his attempts to matriculate for medical education in the United States.

After finishing his secondary education at the African Free School, Smith traveled to Scotland where he was admitted to work toward the B.A. degree, starting in 1831 at the University of Glasgow. He remained there for six years until he earned the B.A. in 1835, the M.A. in 1836, and the M.D. degree in 1837.[7]

Ten years after Smith's achievements in Glasgow, the first black American earned an M.D. degree in the United States: this success story belonged to David John Peck who graduated from the Benjamin Rush Medical College of Chicago in 1847.[8] Following Peck in the United States was John V. deGrasse who earned his degree in 1849. Unlike James McCune Smith, neither Peck nor deGrasse were successful in establishing a practice in the United States and in gaining the respect of whites. Smith, however, did succeed in establishing a large medical practice in New York City with broad based respect from white physicians and scientists.[9]

Against the background of the slave codes and the prevalence of beliefs about the mental inferiority of blacks, it was not surprising to find discrimination and overt resistance to blacks during the nineteenth century wherever they sought medical education in the United States. These kinds of resistances were especially pronounced during the antebellum period.

Early Black Women in Medicine

The first woman to receive a degree in medicine in the United States was Elizabeth Blackwell in 1849. It should come as no surprise that she was a white woman. The degree was conferred upon her by the Geneva Medical College of New York.[10] This event occurred just two years after the first black American, David John Peck, earned an M.D. degree (1847) from the Benjamin Rush Medical College of Chicago.

In spite of the widespread opposition to the presence of women in the profession of medicine, and the comparative freedom from oppression and other privileges normally associated with a white social identity, Blackwell's achievements raises the specter of the additional obstacles faced by women of color who sought access to the profession of medicine. The following quotation is illustrative:

> If Dr. Elizabeth Blackwell, with all the advantages obtaining for an English woman of education, social position, and family was considered "either bad or insane" because "it was so scandalous for a woman to be a doctor," the attitude of certain social groups in conservative sections of this country to the black woman who attained the knowledge and authority to practice medicine can be easily conjectured. One can without difficulty imagine what some of these dark-skinned women physicians must have encountered and endured of prejudice and contempt from one group and of doubt and mistrust from the other. But, happily, in spite of it all, the colored woman physician has won for herself a permanent place in the medical world.[11]

The first black woman to receive an M.D. degree in the United States, Rebecca Lee, was to occur sometime later, earned in 1864 from the New England Female Medical College in Boston, Massachusetts.[12] The second black woman to earn a degree in medicine from a college in the United States was Rebecca Cole who in 1867 graduated from the Women's Medical College of Pennsylvania (now the Medical College of Pennsylvania) in Philadelphia.[13] Then in 1870, Susan Maria Smith McKenney Steward, also a black woman, graduated with a degree in medicine from the New York Medical College and Hospital for Women.[14] It is noteworthy, but not coincidental that these three women were admitted and completed their studies at medical colleges located in states where there were strong sentiments in favor of equal rights for "free Negroes" under the law, and deep movements against social oppression, including the domination of women.[15] For example, up to the conclusion of the Civil War, African Americans were disenfranchised in the United States, except in five New England States, including Massachusetts, and in some political districts of the state of New York.[16] In regard to early antislavery movements among women, Hersh notes the following:

> All the women who were the first to speak out and to organize for woman's rights were abolitionists, as were the men who supported them. Feminism grew naturally out of anti-slavery because the abolitionists' argument for human rights transcended both sex and color, and because the obstacles that women faced made their efforts to work against slavery a feminist consciousness-raising experience.[17]

In addition to the legacy of slavery and the custom of male dominance, many medical school faculties and enabling state legislators from the mid-nineteenth through the first half of the twentieth century were deeply entrenched in racist and sexist beliefs against the emancipation of women from domestic servitude. Moreover, except where there were strong sentiments against oppressive dominance in race and gender relations, the development of women and blacks in the profession of medicine would in all likelihood have been stunted longer than it was.

Racial and Sexual Ghettoes in the History of Medicine

While the historical focus of this study is the period between 1896 and 1965, the previous discussion has shown that patterns of race and sex-related segregation in higher education and the health professions did not begin with this period. Segregation in the profession of medicine and other walks of life that became entrenched with the sanction of law in the early twentieth century had deep roots in the antebellum history of the United States. Harvard University, one of the distinguished institutions of higher education before and since the Civil War exhibited antebellum sentiments among faculty, students, and administrators that symbolized the societal forces contributing to the underdevelopment of African American men and women in medical education and practice. Because of the sociohistorical importance of this citadel of higher learning, and the persistence into the twentieth century of segregationist issues that divided its faculty and students at least as early as 1850, detailed discussion is warranted here.

The Situation of the Harvard Medical School, Class of 1850

Included among the distinguished students admitted to the Harvard Medical School in 1850 were three African Americans; Martin Robinson Delaney, Daniel Laing, Jr., and Isaac H. Snowden. A white woman was considered also for admission, but when she became aware of the deep opposition to a woman student at the college, she withdrew her application.[18]

Delaney, Laing, and Snowden comprised the first group of blacks ever admitted to Harvard. Delaney, however, was clearly the most distinguished because of his pre-admissions activities with abolitionists throughout the northern United States.[19]

Laing and Snowden had received their pre-medical training and financial support from the American Colonization Society and entered Harvard after having given prior consent to serve in Liberia. Therefore it came as no surprise when post-admissions sentiments by Wendall Holmes, its distinguished Dean, suggested that these black students should devote some service, including their internships, in Liberia under the auspices of the American Colonization Society.[20] Laing and Snowden concurred with this idea without question. Delaney, however, refused to go to Liberia insisting that he intended to practice in the United States following graduation. [21] He had applied and gained admission to Harvard without any previous ties to the Colonization Society.[22]

It should be noted that the American Colonization Society was formed in 1816 for the purpose of colonizing "free persons of color" [then in the United States] somewhere outside the country.[23] The Republic of Liberia was created in 1821 on the west coast of Africa for the purpose of colonizing free Negroes.[24] The Harvard Medical College like other institutions in the United States had become a center for training skilled professionals under the immediate auspices of the American Colonization Society.[25] While it was recognized as deviation from custom to admit "colored men" to the medical college, the aim of training physicians for the "colony at Liberia" was considered by the Dean and the faculty as just cause for this innovative activity of the college.[26] Later, however, in the academic year, 1850–51, opposition developed against the presence of the black students.

By 10 December 1850, sentiments had crystallized among white students in support of expelling the three black students.

On Tuesday morning, December 10, the students of Harvard Medical School, already in a state of agitation, assembled (n=116) to consider the question of the three blacks in their midst and the rumor that a woman was soon to join them.... Two series of resolutions were passed and forwarded to the medical faculty. The first series expressed opposition to the admission of a woman and were passed with little or no dissent. The second series protested admission of the three blacks. These were much more controversial and were passed over strong objection. The arguments in these resolutions have a familiar ring: The students (white males) had not been informed (by the faculty) that such a decision had been made, the presence of blacks would cheapen the Harvard medical degree, the quality of education would suffer and the presence of an inferior race was socially offensive.[27]

After receipt of the students' petitions and several faculty meetings, it was decided to permit the black students to complete the first term since they already had tickets for admission to the various courses. With respect to future enrollment, however, Holmes was directed by the medical faculty on December 26 to write the following to the American Colonization Society:

"This experiment had satisfied the medical faculty that the intermixing of the white and black races in their lecture rooms is distasteful to a large portion of the class and injurious to the interests of the school."[28]

Following this statement by Holmes, all three students were dismissed by March of 1851. Laing, however, went on to matriculate and earn his M.D. degree at Dartmouth College, 1854. Snowden subsequently reapplied at Harvard and was rejected once more. There was no documentation that he ever earned the M.D. degree. It was not until 1869 that the Harvard Medical School produced its first black doctor, Edwin Clarence Joseph Turpin Howard.[29]

In regard to Delaney, one source claimed that he returned to Pittsburgh and completed his medical education through an apprenticeship.[30] While it was not established that he ever earned an M.D. degree through a formal institution of higher education, he apparently practiced medicine for a period in and around Pittsburgh. With the addition of sexist biases, black women whose interests turned to medicine faced similar obstacles in their attempts to gain access to medical schools, complete the training programs and establish their practices.

Women Physicians Needed, No Blacks Need Apply

The Women's Medical College of Pennsylvania was established in 1850 for the purpose of educating women physicians. This development was an encouraging sign in a society that had become deeply entrenched in beliefs and values about proper places and roles for women, not including the profession of medicine nor the right to vote. There were widespread beliefs throughout Europe and the United States during the mid-nineteenth century that "...a woman's place is in the home."[31]

At this period, for many, marriage was a woman's only chance to escape from deathly idleness. An unmarried woman of thirty years was an old maid and unless of wealthy family, condemned to the ill- paid and despised work of governess as her sole source of "independent" support. No profession was open to her. There was no woman in any Government office, even in secretarial work. Even nursing was disorganized and was considered disreputable until Florence Nightingale founded the School of Nursing in 1860. She published her "Notes on Nursing" in 1859 and advised and aided the Royal Commission on the sanitary state of the British Army in India during 1863 when she advocated the incapacitation of the wounded soldier.[32]

Many women continued to succumb to these sexist constraints well into the twentieth century. But signs of discontent began to appear toward the turn of the century as a few outspoken women started to demand equal rights, seek higher education, and strike for recognition in society.[33] Clearly, discrimination against access of women to medical education and practice affected black and white women alike, but black women were additionally oppressed and degraded as a consequence of race discrimination. It should also be noted that the content and emphasis in the above quotation from Percy may be more symbolic of white European and Euro-American middle-class culture than African American beliefs and values about the propriety of place and roles for women in society. It is acknowledged also that the Medical College of Pennsylvania (formerly the Women's Medical College) was distinguished early in its history (post-Civil War) along with a few other historically white medical schools by the practice of admitting women physicians. However, according to a *Crisis Magazine* account of the experiences of Virginia May Alexander, a black woman and 1925 graduate of the Medical College of Pennsylvania, getting in and through the medical school program up through the early twentieth century was not devoid of discriminatory treatment of black students:

The difficulty there...was not simply that of money. The Women's Medical College of Pennsylvania at that time and perhaps even now distinctly did not want to encourage colored students.... There was one professor who took especial delight and pains in retelling to his classes, where there were colored students, every discreditable, dirty and insulting story about colored people he could think of; and when on complaint the Dean had to interfere, the professor simply walked on and lectured these [black] girls about trying to get above their people. It did not make any difference what they tried to accomplish, they must remember that they were still Negroes.[34]

Substantively, the latter part of these quoted materials probably do not distinguish the classroom experiences of black women from those of black men in pursuit of medical education in predominantly white medical schools under separatism. It is worthy of note, however, that being in a medical college for women in the state of Pennsylvania, where there were Quakers and other groups strongly in favor of the abolition of slavery, there was no assurance of freedom for black women from the racially motivated degradation ceremonies of whites.

The Calling(s) of Women in Medicine

According to Pauline Dinkens, a 1919 black woman graduate of the Women's Medical College, "women serving women" was one of the most important needs to be filled by women physicians.[35] Although Dinkens did not make explicit reference to the early-twentieth-century social expectations that women should be restrained in the presence of unfamiliar males, especially with regard to personal bodily matters, the customs of the period suggested support for her statement of the importance of women serving women. Brown's recent analysis of *Southern Honor*[36] and the observations of widespread developments of intimate relations among women illustrates the comforts they sought and found through each other as an adjustment to life in a paternalistic society in which they often felt estranged from men.

> ...Reasons for the development [of intimacies among women] included the recurring cycles of confinement owing to disease and childbirth, bodily concerns that modest women could not so easily share with members of the opposite sex.... As nurses and confidantes ministering to each other's health, they were in touch with others on matters of heart and head as well. In ways only women could appreciate, death in the family and among those nearby tended to bring survivors together. Like the rituals of the wedding, the rites of the funeral were times when women could express themselves in public without restraint. The occasion represented a contrast with the decorum expected of them in male company.

In addition to the need for close intimate relations among women and the extension of this need to women physicians, women seemed also to have a greater preference than their men counterparts for medical missionary practices and pediatrics. Dinkens noted, in a letter from her to Martha Tracy, dated 9 September 1919 that:

> More and more I see the need of social medicine. It seems to me that male physi-

cians do not stress this enough. I do not want to be in this country many years, but while I am here, I do want to put all my energy in this work, as far as possible.[37]

Here, Dinkens's complaint about the omission of emphases on "social medicine" in the medical practices of male physicians points indirectly to an actual difference between men and women in kinds of practices established between the late nineteenth and mid-twentieth centuries. Medical missionary services seemed to be the major indicator of social medicine of concern to Dinkens. What follows first will be a discussion of gender differences in preferences for missionary services followed by the development of specialties in pediatrics.

Gender Differences in the Missionary Zeal

Earlier in this discussion, the interest of the American Colonization Society was noted with reference to the training of blacks for practices in Liberia and other assignments on continental Africa. It is worthy of note that far more black women than black men in medicine expressed interests early in their educational development and careers in devoting some part or all of their careers in medicine to serve the health care needs of the poor abroad, especially in Africa. In an analysis of the life and work of Lulu Cecilia Fleming, M.D., it was noted that young black men were not attracted to Africa nor to missionary commitments as their women counterparts.[38]

> Young black men were not drawn to Africa, possibly because there was a great demand among black churches for better educated pastors. "But," he added, "it will be easy to find fairly educated colored young women for all the primary schools we shall care to establish among the Congo Tribes." He reported that in one school in Georgia, over 200 such young women were "preparing for teaching and preaching...[and] more than half of the unmarried women are eager to go."[39]

Black men physicians were more likely than women to select stateside work and to combine their medical practices with other forms of business enterprise for profit.

In many instances, such as in the case of Matilda Evans, M.D., of Columbia, South Carolina, medical humanitarian interests found expression through ministering to the health care needs of the African American poor. The following passage, exemplary of the missionary spirit of Matilda A. Evans, appeared in *The Palmetto Leader*, a local newspaper in Columbia South Carolina on 22 March 1930:

> The exercise of her missionary spirit and her interest in the people's health gener-

ally have found substantial expression in her concern for playgrounds for children and places of recreation for older ones.... Truly is she one who lives in a house by the side of the road and is a friend of man.[40]

While Evans did not get to Africa, the record showed that she successfully ministered to thousands of her people in South Carolina.[41] Like the dedication of Evans, the humanistic concerns of other black women in medicine implied a concept of missionary work that went far beyond going abroad to practice medicine in the service of ex-slaves in Liberia and other members of the poor and dispossessed.

Similar missionary zeal is shown in the biography of Georgia Patton Washington, an 1893 graduate of Meharry Medical College and the first "woman of color to be given authority to practice medicine and surgery in Tennessee.[42]

On May 5th following her graduation in medicine, she sailed for Africa, her chosen field of labor, as a self-supporting medical missionary. On August 15th she writes from Monrovia as follows: "For the first few days after my arrival, the surroundings looked very discouraging for my professional work. On examining my first case, remarks made by the natives were: 'Patients in his condition will never get well; we always expect them to die. You may as well give him up; he will die.'" After careful treatment and watching for two months he was able to leave his bed, and finally went to his work. The next two cases were also considered to be hopeless, yet both recovered. Later, Dr. Patton writes, "I have treated over one hundred cases, and have lost four." Notwithstanding failure of her health, she continued at Monrovia two years, doing faithful and satisfactory work, when she was compelled to leave for her native land.[43]

Comparative studies of archives,[44] interview materials on career objectives, and documents on practices actually developed, repeatedly show black women physicians as more sensitive, nurturing, and self-sacrificing of personal comforts and material gain when compared to men physicians in the interests of delivering high quality health care for the poor and downtrodden in the United States and in Africa. While sexist discrimination against interests by women in surgery and other highly technical specialties helps to account for their overrepresentation in other areas, like pediatrics, the latter specialty along with missionary work also permitted women to be nurturing and practice what some called "social medicine."

The Preference for a Specialty in Pediatrics: The Significance of Gender

Pediatrics was another area of practice in which black women physicians seemed to show more interest than their black men counterparts. The differential interest in pediatrics among women could have been an indirect expression of their missionary zeal, as described above; and/or a legacy of the well-known historical background of women in midwifery as well as their personal preferences and social expectations, albeit sexist, that they would be naturally inclined toward domestic matters, such as the bearing and nurturing of children. This is suggested in the following quotation:

> Pediatrics is one specialty into which many women tend to gravitate. It is seen as a sort of women's job. Obstetrics-Gynecology may be another. Yet my reasons for choosing pediatrics had little to do with any stereotype. I was about equally pulled among internal medicine, surgery, and pediatrics. But I had long range plans for a home and family, and I love children. Pediatrics was compatible with that set of facts. It was a perfectly conscious decision. Thus it would seem that a woman's domestic needs and proclivities do have a powerful determining influence on her career choice and are thereafter a factor in her successful functioning in that career.[45]

While the spirit of outreach and nurturing was clearly expressed through the missionary zeal and concern about child and maternal health among black women physicians, there were limits on the ways in which they expressed their health care interests, at least in the United States. While going into the countryside to visit homes of peasants and deliver services was not unknown in African medical missionary work and among midwives in the rural United States, this practice was the exception rather than the rule among black women physicians, especially in urban areas of the United States.

Gender and the Omission of House Calls: Excursus on the Professional Significance of Rules of Etiquette

The relative absence of black women physicians among users of house calls, a technique most commonly observed among country doctors in the practice of medicine, was an unexpected finding which grew out of my studies of protocols of physician interviews and medical school archives. A country doctor, a topic more fully discussed in chapter 9, is an individual trained in scientific medicine and related approaches to health care, but is distinguished by a practice that is primarily rural and extensively dependent on the uses of house calls as a means of health-care delivery. Each of these factors was the exception, rather than the rule in the professional organization of black women physicians in this study.

The preponderance of black women physicians observed in this study were urban-based practitioners and, with few exceptions, reported no use of house calls. The reasons for the these omissions are not clear, but the available data do provide some clues.

Medical Missionaries: Etiquette Takes a Holiday

One set of exceptions to the observed omissions of house calls were the practices of women medical missionaries in Africa. Exceptions in this regard were, in part, related to the pervasiveness of agrarian settlements and ways of life of the people. Africa, south of the Sahara, including the Congo (now Zaire) was primarily rural with agricultural economies during the late nineteenth and early twentieth century. Even though extensive urban development has occurred since the turn of the century, public health problems are still widespread, and many of the pressures for medical missionaries in the early twentieth century were closely related to the need for physicians with public health interests to help withstand the devastating affects of epidemics. It was in this kind of practice where black women physicians were more prevalent than men.

Rules of Etiquette: Calling at Homes of Strangers

While illness and the need for health care appealed to the sensitivities of all trained physicians, men and women alike, there were gender differences in interactions with women and men patients. In addition, the socioecological place where illness behavior was expressed, such as a private home, and the local and/or regional beliefs and rules for gender-related deportment in public places were key factors helping to determine the performance of medical practices by men and women. For example, from at least the early eighteenth century through World War II, it was acceptable for men to be seen in public places with or without a companion, whether in work-related or other daily living activities, but unescorted women in public places were frowned upon.[46]

Among the eighty-three sets of records on black women in medicine studied through the archives of the Medical College of Pennsylvania, there was no evidence of uses of house calls among them. It should also be noted that there was no evidence that any of these women ever established residences or practices in rural residential settings after earning the M.D. degree. The significance of the latter finding is partly signified by the fact that "country doctors" were (and still are) the major users of house calls, a technique which many women refrained from using, perhaps in honor of rules of etiquette against the public appearance of a woman at the home of a stranger at selected times of day and/ or appearances in public places without an escort. Secondly, perhaps because of the considerable mileage between private homes and doctors' offices in rural areas and small towns, the house call, which is especially well-suited to these relatively isolated residential settings, delimited rural medical practices by women physicians. Instead, public health physicians (usually men), local midwives, and other practitioners of traditional medicine were left to provide the needed health care services.

In addition to the foregoing interpretation of late-nineteenth- and early-twentieth-century mores related to gender and appearances in public places, the absence of black women physicians among country doctors in the United States may also be due to the following reason: most of the eighty-three women for whom records were relatively complete and collected for this study through the archives of the Medical College of Pennsylvania (August 1988–February 1989) were born in large cities between 1900 and 1965. Moreover, upon graduation, many returned to those areas or related subregions of metropolitan areas for practice.

A Further Interpretive Note on Etiquette

Sociologically, behavior is structured by the customs current in a society during a given sociohistorical period. It seems also reasonable to conclude that general rules for proper conduct in public places, such as those pertaining to gender-related manners of deportment, will not be altered nor diminished in importance during a given generation merely because of individual attainment of professional standing, for example, in the professions of law, medicine, nursing, or education. In fact, in various studies of social mobility, inequality, and etiquette, it is suggested that expectations of compliance with rules of etiquette become more (rather than less) intense with each successful climb up the social ladder.[47] It is partly for these reasons that I turned to books of etiquette of the late-nineteenth- and early-twentieth-century United States in my attempt to account for the omission of house calls among women physicians in the practice of medicine.

In the history of rules for behavior in public places, there are discernible differences related to gender identity and rules for making "calls" at the homes of other persons. Although no descriptions or discussions were found specific to house calls of physicians, historical descriptions of general rules of etiquette by gender, status relations (such as family versus friend, close acquaintance versus stranger), and other variables lend support to the hypothesis that sociocultural constraints shaped by gender-related values and beliefs of the period may have inhibited the use of the technique of house calls by women in medicine. For example, in her 1914 *Encyclopedia of Etiquette*,[48] Emily Holt showed that while men were given and expected to take wide-ranging liberties with house calls, whether formal or informal, women were considerably restricted by time of day and related circumstances under which a "call" could be made. This practice was especially, but not exclusively followed when making a call at the home of a stranger or a business acquaintance.

There is no claim here of a direct relationship between gender-related rules of etiquette and constraints on house calls among black women physicians. It is hypothesized, however, although not conducive to test through available data, that gender identity may override professional identity in regard to rules of etiquette for conduct in public places. Secondly, it is hypothesized that the behavior of women and men in public places will, with the exception of error variation due to lack of training in rules of etiquette, defiance against local custom, or other intervening factors, tend to adhere to rules for public decorum and deportment of the generation or sociohistorical period, with little or no deviation from cultural norms as a consequence of occupational or professional training. It seems reasonable, however, as suggested by Holt (1914)[49] and Eichler (1921)[50], that public expectations for individual compliance with rules of etiquette will increase with individual successes in status ascendancy.

Conclusions

Gender, the configuration of sociosexual identity that helps to frame the status and role sets of each individual, intrudes in all domains of social life. The development of careers and practices of medicine is no exception. Similar statements can be made about race. As shown in this chapter, racial identity and the social construction of the "color line" have been the great overarching barriers to the successful development of careers in medicine among African American people. While gender has been an important factor—both a creator of opportunities, (especially for women by, for example, female patients who showed preferences for women physicians), and on the other hand, an object of discrimination—race in most instances of individual careers and institutional design (such as hospital and clinic practices), appears to be the overriding structural factor that produced differential successes among men and women physicians.

The next chapter on "The Significance of Physician Access to Hospitals" depicts a variety of attempts, some small and sporadic, some large-scale and systematic, to rise above the degrading experiences associated with the putative health care provided through ghetto wards. In addition to the importance of these facilities as a means of achieving clinical experiences through which blacks could cultivate specialties in medicine, the segregated hospitals and wards were both a response to race discrimination, and symbolic of the limits of the commitments that whites were willing to make to the intervention systems needed to prevent illness and enhance the health and welfare of black Americans. Many of the self-help efforts of blacks were valiant and successful. A preponderance of their ventures were feeble and underfunded from the start, with little chance of success against the great odds of racist oppression. Yet, the full story is worthy of careful study. We turn in the next chapter to the calling and the problems of hospitals owned and operated by blacks.

Notes

1. Sara W. Brown, "Colored Women Physicians," *The Southern Workman* vol. 52, no. 12 (Dec. 1923), p. 592.
2. Rosalyn P. Sterling, "Female Surgeons: The Dawn of a New Era," in Claude H. Organ, Jr. and Margaret M. Kosiba (eds.), *A Century of Black Surgeons: The U.S.A. Experience*, vol. 2, pp. 587–588 (Norman, OK: Transcript Press, 1987).
3. See for example, Darlene Clark Hine, "Co-Laborers in the Work of the Lord: 19th Century Black Women Physicians," in Ruth J. Abram (ed.), *Send Us a Lady Physician: Women Doctors in America, 1835–1920*, pp. 107–120 (New York: W.W. Norton and Company, 1985). See also W. Montague Cobb, "Progress and Portents for the Negro in Medicine," *The Crisis*, vol. 55, no. 4 (Apr. 1948), pp. 107–122.
4. Grace Harrison, "Hubbard Hospital and Meharry Medical College for Negroes, Nashville, Tennessee" (unpublished Master's Thesis, University of Chicago, Mar. 1945). See also Gary King, "The Supply and Distribution of Black Physicians in the United States: 1900–1970," *Western Journal of Black Studies* vol. 4, no. 1 (Spring 1980), pp. 21–39.
5. Regina Markell Morantz, Cynthia Stodola Pomerleau, and Carol Hansen Fenichel (eds.), *In Her Own Words: Oral Histories of Women Physicians* (New Haven, CT: Yale University Press, 1982); Mary Roth Walsh, *Doctors Wanted, No Women Need Apply: Sexual Barriers in the Medical Profession, 1835-1975* (New Haven, CT: Yale University Press, 1977); and Dorothy Sterling (ed.), *We Are Your Sisters: Black Women in the Nineteenth Century* (New York: W.W. Norton and Company, 1984), pp. 397–450.

6. W. Montague Cobb, "James McCune Smith: First Black American M.D.," *Journal of the National Medical Association*, vol. 73 (suppl. 1981), p. 1205.

7. Ibid.

8. Ibid., p. 1206.

9. Ibid.

10. W. Montague Cobb, "Delaney the Redoubtable," *Journal of the National Medical Association,* vol. 73 (suppl. 1981), p. 1206.

11. Brown, "Colored Women Physicians," p. 593.

12. Archive on Black Women Physicians, file K–Z, Medical College of Pennsylvania, August 1988.

13. Ibid., file A-J, Letter from Ida J. Draeger, Librarian of the Medical College of Pennsylvania, to Miss Virginia Warner, St. Louis, MS. Also see the article by Brown, "Colored Women Physicians," pp. 580–593.

14. Archive on Black Women Physicians, file K–Z, *op. cit.*

15. See, for example, J. William Frost (ed.), *The Quaker Origins of Antislavery* (Norwood, PA: Norwood Editions, 1980). This book documents early antislavery movements in the state of Pennsylvania. See also Jean R. Soderlund, *Quakers and Slavery: A Divided Spirit* (Princeton, NJ: Princeton University Press, 1985).

16. Arnold Rose, *The Negro American,* with a foreword by Gunnar Myrdal (Boston: The Beacon Press, 1948), p. 141.

17. Blanche Glassman Hersh, "Am I Not A Woman and a Sister? Abolitionist Beginnings of Nineteenth-Century Feminism," p. 252 in Lewis Perry and Michael Fellman (eds.), *Antislavery Reconsidered: New Perspectives on the Abolitionists* (Baton Rouge, LA: Louisiana State University Press, 1979).

18. Werner Sollors, Thomas A. Underwood, and Caldwell Titcomb (eds.), *Varieties of Black Experience at Harvard: An Anthology* (Cambridge, MA: Harvard University Department of Afro-American Studies, 1986), pp. 21, 25. See also Doris Y. Wilkinson, "The 1850 Harvard Medical School Dispute and The Admission of African-American Students." *Harvard Library Bulletin,* vol. 3, no. 3 (Fall 1992), pp. 13–27.

19. W. Montague Cobb, "James McCune Smith," pp. 1205–06.

20. Ibid., p. 1206.

21. Ibid., p. 1206.

22. Sollors et al., pp. 23–24.

23. William Jay, *Inquiry into the Character and Tendency of the American Colonization and American Anti-Slavery Societies* (New York: Negro Universities Press [1838]1969), p. 15.

24. Charles S. Johnson, *Bitter Canaan: The Story of the Negro Republic,* with a new introduction by John Stanfield (New Brunswick, NJ: Transaction Publishers, 1987).

25. Sollors et al., p. 22.

26. Ibid.

27. Ibid., p. 25.

28. Cobb,"James McCune Smith," p. 1205.

29. Sollors et al., p. 27. See also W. Montague Cobb, "The Black American in Medicine," *Journal of the National Medical Association,* vol. 73 (suppl. 1981), p. 1207.

30. Joseph E. Harris (ed.), *Global Dimensions of the African Diaspora* (Washington, DC: Howard University Press, 1982), p. 145.

31. "Early Black Women Physicians," *Women and Health*, vol. 5, no. 3 (Fall 1980), p. 1.

32. Percy Ward Laidler and Michael Gelfand, *South Africa/Its Medical History, 1652–1898: A Medical and Social Study* (Capetown: C. Struik (PTY) LTD., 1971), p. 341.
33. "Early Black Women Physicians," p. 1.
34. "Can a Colored Woman Be a Physician?" *The Crisis Magazine,* vol. 40, no. 2 (February 1933), pp. 33–34.
35. See the Questionnaire to Alumnae of the Women's Medical College of Pennsylvania completed by Pauline Dinkens, File on Black Women Physicians, A–J, MCP Archives, August 1988.
36. Bertram Wyatt Brown, *Southern Honor: Ethics and Behavior in the Old South* (New York: Oxford University Press, 1982), pp. 247–248.
37. See the letter from Pauline Dinkens to Martha Tracy, 9 September 1919, File on Pauline Dinkens, Collection on Black Women Physicians, A–J, MCP Archives, August 1988.
38. "Zaire Missionary Pioneer: Lulu Cecilia Fleming, M.D., 1862–1899" (Valley Forge, Pennsylvania: International Ministries, ABC/United States, n.d.). This document is available in the Black Women Physicians Project, files A–J, MCP Archives, August 1988.
39. Ibid., pp. 2–3, and 7.
40. "Noted Physician and Surgeon, Humanitarian, Outstanding Citizen of Columbia." *The Palmetto Leader,* Saturday, 22 March 1930, pp. 1 and 8. Available in the MCP Archives, Black Women Physicians, Files A–J.
41. A.B. Caldwell, *History of the American Negro,* South Carolina ed. (Atlanta, Georgia: A.B. Caldwell Publishing Company, 1919), pp. 393–396. Also see the file on Matilda A. Evans, Black Women Physicians Project, MCP Archives, Box A–J, 1988.
42. G. W. Hubbard, "Dr. Georgia E. L. Patton Washington," *The Christian Educator*, 12, 1900–01, p. 5; see also the file on Georgia Patton Washington, Black Women Physicians Project, MCP Archives, file box K–Z, 1988.
43. Ibid.
44. Black Women Physicians Project, MCP, Archives, file boxes A–Z, 1988.
45. Gertrude T. Hunter, "Pediatrician," *Annals of the New York Academy of Sciences,* vol. 208 (15 March 1973), pp. 38–39.
46. Hersh, "Am I Not a Women and a Sister," pp. 265, 280.
47. Emily Holt, *Encyclopedia of Etiquette: A Book of Manners in Everyday Use* (New York: Doubleday, Page and Co., 1914), p. 18.
48. Ibid.
49. Ibid.
50. Eichler.

4

The Significance of Physician Access to Hospitals

The segregated hospital, born of the needs of the Negro patient and the Negro doctor, began to fulfill its destiny well before the turn of the century. Invariably, an unpretentious facility, plagued by problems of funding, it was nevertheless the prime agency in the development of the pioneer black surgeon and a majority of those who followed.
—Maynard (undated)[1]

Desegregation has been the undoing of black medicine.... When they desegregated, all [black] patients deserted the hospital, the doctors deserted the hospital, and everybody went his own way.
—Thomas (1986)[2]

From at least as early as 1650 to the passage of the amended Hill-Burton Act in 1965, there developed various customs, laws, and court decisions in the United States to regulate interaction between blacks and whites. These forces effectively segregated black and white relations in nearly all walks of life. Although slavery, the black codes, and Jim Crow had their own oppressive effects, the years between 1832 (which saw the founding of the first hospital for blacks in Savannah, Georgia) and the amended Hill-Burton Act of 1965 marked the heights of separatism in health care practices in the United States. This period saw the rise by 1928 of at least 183 African American owned and operated hospitals representing part of an attempt by blacks to respond proactively to separatism by developing their own health care institutions.[3]

Segregated hospitals were more prevalent and accessible to black physicians before the turn of the twentieth century and continued to be up through 1965.[4] The prevalence of segregated facilities in the Southeastern United States was accounted for, in part, by racial separatism, and the greater density of black physicians and black populations in these states. Also influential were the initiatives taken by blacks, some white philanthropists and other interest groups in establishing hospitals for medical practice and training schools for African American nurses.

It should be noted that among black physicians there was widespread objection to segregation and exclusion from access to opportunities to have their patients admitted to other hospitals such that they could practice medicine regardless of race. But as Myrdal suggested, with segregation there was also opportunity for professionals and other middle- and upper-class African Americans.

> The entire Negro middle and upper class becomes caught in an ideological dilemma. On the one hand, they find that the caste wall blocks their economic and social opportunities. On the other hand, they have at the same time a vested interest in racial segregation since it gives them what opportunities they have.[5]

Some hospitals were also established for blacks in the northern United States, for example, the Provident Hospitals in Chicago and Baltimore and the Frederick Douglass Hospital of Philadelphia. By 1965, the number of black owned and/or operated hospitals in the United States had dwindled to less than eighty. This chapter develops a political economic analysis and explanation of the rise and fall of hospitals owned and/or operated by African Americans, from one in 1832, to 183 in 1928, to less than 80 in 1965.[6]

Incentives for the Development of Black Owned and Operated Hospitals

There were few specialties in medicine for which black graduates of medical schools could gain admission to hospital residencies before World War II. As a consequence, most black physicians who completed medical school between 1871 and World War II were limited to internships in family medicine, midwifery/ obstetrics, gynecology, or pediatrics. These internships were usually acquired through faculty-supervised experiences within the facilities of a few black owned and operated teaching hospitals in the United States. Most notable among these teaching hospitals were the Howard University Hospital (formerly, the Freedmen's Hospital) 1866–present; the Provident Hospitals in Chicago (1891–1988) and in Baltimore (1894–1986); the Homer G. Phillips

Hospital (formerly, St. Louis Hospital No. II), St. Louis, Missouri, 1937–present; the Flint Goodridge Hospital, New Orleans, Louisiana, 1901–1985; the Frederick Douglass Hospital and Training School of Philadelphia, 1895. Frederick Douglass merged with the Mercy Nurses Training School in 1907 to form the Mercy Douglass Hospital and Training School, which closed in 1973; Hubbard Hospital in Nashville, Tennessee (1910–1994); and the Hospital of the Veterans Administration Medical Center in Tuskegee (1923–present, originally named "The Hospital for Sick and Injured Colored War Veterans").[7]

According to Dr. William A. Cleland of Durham, North Carolina, "there were only forty-two slots" in 1934 for black medical interns in the United States.[8] Of those slots, Howard University absorbed the top twenty black graduates of medical schools in that year, and Meharry Medical College took the majority of the remainder.[9] It should also be pointed out that the School for Midwifery at Tuskegee Institute helped to provide training in obstetrics and gynecology for black physicians who could not obtain residency appointments during the 1930s.[10]

In the training of physicians, regardless of race or sex, access to hospitals was especially important for the development of a specialty in surgery.[11] Surgery requires the antiseptic control of germs that can be maximized in the laboratory-like conditions of hospital operating rooms.

Secondly, until recently, white physicians in white owned and/or operated hospitals exercised tight control over these facilities for residency training and other opportunities in the development of the profession of medicine. According to Hubert Eaton, one of the oldest black physicians in Wilmington, North Carolina, "white doctors have always guarded operating rooms in hospitals."[12] While blacks had little difficulty getting residencies for training in internal medicine and obstetrics, which could be achieved through most hospitals including those controlled by blacks, access to opportunities for residencies in surgery were more difficult to realize.

Power and Politics of White Sponsors of Black Physicians

The influence of white significant others, or "sponsors," on the medical education and careers of blacks was clear: They stood between black physicians, especially those with interests in surgery and the supportive services of hospitals that were important to the successful performance of surgical practices. Helping to frame the structure of power of white physicians and their influences on the practices of medicine by blacks were the beliefs and values of "cracker culture" pertaining to race-related status differentiation and the corresponding rules for social interaction.

"Cracker culture" is a term used by Hill and McCall[13] to refer to a white Southern point of view that included the following norms or rules for behavior:

> Negroes must assume roles of deference, subordination, obedience and strict adherence to the "cracker" etiquette. Custom requires a Negro to have a white "sponsor" who will relate him to the white community. Both concrete services such as cooking, housekeeping and babysitting, and evidence of respect, obedience and deference are expected as expressions of gratitude for this sponsorship. Correspondingly, Negroes who maintain economic relationships with whites expect sponsorship as part of the contract.

In the context of cracker culture, these rules meant that blacks were compelled in many walks of life, including the professions and businesses to make every effort to establish a working relationship with a white sponsor to facilitate their own social mobility.

The constraints on blacks that occurred as consequences of their conditioning to live by the rules of cracker culture were not the only symbols of the powers of white physicians in hierarchies of access to medical practice and hospital privileges. It is ironic, but consistent with *herrenvolk* democratic beliefs, discussed in chapter 2, that in selected instances, white physicians used their knowledge and skills to achieve outcomes that enhanced the skills and medical practices of black physicians while simultaneously reinforcing the walls of segregation. A black physician in North Carolina gives an example of this situation by citing the experiences of a black colleague who, while doing his residency at Lincoln Hospital (that was established by blacks in Durham, North Carolina in 1903), received training and "sponsorship of the faculty of Duke" University Hospital, a white owned and operated facility.[14]

> They [the white medical school faculty of Duke] were trying to upgrade the care of the black community on a segregated basis. They helped him [the black resident] get his credentials so he could take the board, a bastardly arrangement at best because he was not a part of a major teaching program. But he [the black resident] was quite bright, applied himself, and passed his board with no difficulty.[15]

Where Black Owned and Operated Hospitals were the Only Medical Centers in Town

Unlike the other towns in this study, Tuskegee, Alabama and Georgetown, South Carolina were distinguished by having only one privately owned and operated hospital before 1954. In addition to admitting black patients without the prerequisite of a white sponsor, these hospitals were owned and/or operated by blacks: that was the John A. Andrew Hospital, 1908–1986 in Tuskegee, Alabama and the Sarah Haynes Hospital, 1930–1956 in Georgetown, South Carolina. The other inpatient facility in the city of Tuskegee was the Veterans Administration Hospital. To help frame the following discussion, it is worthy of emphasis that there were no white owned and/or operated hospitals in either Tuskegee or Georgetown during the periods noted above.

The Veterans Administration Hospital of Tuskegee, originally named the "Hospital for Sick and Injured Colored War Veterans," was dedicated for service on 12 February 1923.[16] It grew out of the system of racial segregation and discrimination in the United States where the rules of separatism of the period precluded treatment for African Americans, including "Negro soldiers" in racially mixed hospitals in the South. Secondly, in spite of segregation, the U.S. Department of Defense took a firm position that it wanted special care given to all war veterans, regardless of race. To help achieve this goal, the Tuskegee Hospital for Sick and Colored Veterans was constructed in 1923 solely for the care of over 300,000 black veterans in the South.[17]

One indication of the entrenchment of the "color line" and the attempts by whites to oppress any attempts by blacks to achieve autonomy in the development and management of institutions for their betterment is shown by the reactions of white Alabamans to the announcement of a Veterans Administration Hospital for blacks in that state. One might have thought that being embedded in the faculty of a "historically black" college, Tuskegee, would have provided some protection for black physicians and other staff of the hospital against the savagery of hooded white horsemen. Such protection, however, was not there for John A. Kenney, M.D., in Tuskegee in 1922:

> In 1922, with plans consummated for the construction of a hospital for Negro veterans of World War I on the grounds of the Tuskegee Institute, a cabal of local white citizens, sensing material benefits to be gained, exercised their political power and demanded a white professional staff for the new facility. This was strongly opposed by Dr. Kenney who sought a black staff for the institution. His inflexible stand led to a violent reaction by the Ku Klux Klan, with the burning of fiery crosses on the grounds of the Institute and in front of Dr. Kenney's residence. Terror, threat, intimidation, the odious trinity of the K.K.K. began to mount. Warned that his life was in danger, Dr. Kenney dispatched his family to the North and left shortly thereafter to join them in New Jersey at the home of Dr. George Cannon, Sr., the Chairman of the Executive Board of the National Medical Association (NMA). The matter was fought through the NMA, the NAACP [National Association for the Advancement of Colored People] and other black organiza-

tions, with the final decision made by the government for the installation of a Negro professional staff.[18]

In this regard, it is interesting to note that even though there was a large number of whites living in Tuskegee, neither a public nor a private hospital owned and operated by whites ever developed in that city during the first half of the twentieth century.

During the period between 1896 and 1965, most of the whites in Tuskegee were poor.[19] Although not necessarily poorer than blacks, they did not have the resources to establish and financially consume the services of a hospital for the exclusive use of white Tuskegeeans.

It should be noted that whites did attempt to found in the late 1940s a hospital in Tuskegee established to serve their own interests. It did not, however, survive because of a lack of funds and its failure to meet state and federal hospital standards.

Among the peculiar circumstances leading to the founding of the John A. Andrew Hospital, the wealth of blacks was not paramount. Crucial, however, was a donation made in 1913 by Mrs. Elizabeth Mason of Boston as a memorial to her grandfather, the honorable John Albion Andrew, Civil War governor of Massachusetts.[20] The money was originally donated to fund a hospital for training nurses at the Tuskegee Institute. It was through that donation that construction of the John A. Andrew Hospital was completed and dedicated in 1913 and sustained over time.[21] It should be noted that Tuskegee Institute (now Tuskegee University) actually began health services for students in 1881 with the inception of the Institute. The first hospital on the grounds was established in 1900.[22]

It is also worthy of note that white doctors in Tuskegee, unlike those in many other localities observed in this study, were compelled to do more house calls than black physicians to deliver babies and provide other kinds of primary care for their patients. This phenomenon resulted, in large measure from the fact that white doctors did not have a hospital where they could take white patients in Tuskegee.[23] When a patient of a white doctor required hospitalization, the practice was to take the patient to the Montgomery Community Hospital, forty miles south in the city of Montgomery, Alabama. Another option for white doctors was the Auburn Medical Center, about fifteen miles southwest of Tuskegee. These black/white differences in the logistics of hospital location, and racially restricted access, whether perceived or externally enforced, represents two of the indicators of the high costs of racial segregation.

In spite of the presence of the John A. Andrew Memorial Hospital and the willingness of the black medical directors to admit white patients, and/or to permit white doctors to have their white patients admitted, only a few white doctors availed themselves of that opportunity during the period of separatism. Instead, most chose to take their patients many miles outside the Tuskegee area in order to sustain segregation or avoid "race mixing."

"Back Porch Nursing" and Rural Health Clinics:
An Unusual Feature of Health Service Delivery through
the John A. Andrew Hospital

At its inception, the John A. Andrew Memorial Hospital did not have an outpatient clinic for the delivery of medical services. This is to say, there were no outpatient medical services based in the hospital complex itself. There was an emergency room service, operated on a limited basis. Most patients treated on an emergency basis were either released immediately, or admitted for a short stay on an inpatient basis.

The John A. Andrew Hospital was further distinguished from other hospitals in the country by its outreach and decentralized clinic services through rural households, small churches, and back rooms of stores located in communities in the surrounding rural countryside of Tuskegee Institute. These country clinics were primarily focused on birthing infants, maternal health care and the treatment of disorders that did not require hospitalization. Most of the patients from the communities served would come to the outreach facility, sometimes called "back porch nursing," rather than the hospital, John A. Andrews, in the city of Tuskegee.[24] "Back porch nursing" got its name from the actual use of back porches of rural households to examine and treat persons before the development of a hospital at Tuskegee. Tuskegee Institute was founded in 1881. To help upgrade the quality of care that could be given by these pioneers of "community" and home-delivered nursing care, Tuskegee established in 1892 a two-year program of training for "back porch nursing."[25] The hospital in Tuskegee was primarily used for delivery of births, and for acute or intensive care that could not be delivered at home or in the country clinics. Secondly, because of the small number of doctors at the John A. Andrew Hospital, staff medical doctors seldom made house calls. Instead, they took referrals when necessary from the "back porch nurses," and otherwise supervised their work with the poor and underserved, forming a network of dedicated health care servants.[26] This arrangement was in contrast to the practices of physicians and the management of black-operated hospitals elsewhere in the South. In other localities (outside Tuskegee), it was quite common, especially in small towns, to observe frequent uses of house calls by physicians, as means of delivering health care services.

Desegregation and the Challenges of Competitive Hospital Services

The Supreme Court decision of 1954, that declared the idea of "separate but equal" inherently unconstitutional encouraged the intensification of efforts by blacks to acquire equal treatment under the laws of the United States. With the 1965 amendments to the Hill-Burton Act of 1948, prohibiting any further use of federal funds to build segregated hospitals, increasing numbers of black physicians began to refer patients to previously all-white hospitals and sought, as well, staff positions along with surgical privileges in those facilities. The decade of change in law and custom between 1954 and 1965 spelled the end of the major social, cultural, and legal incentives for the development and preservation of black owned and operated hospitals. As a consequence, the numbers have declined sharply and steadily since.

While there has been a broad decline of black owned and operated hospitals since mid-century, some of the extant hospitals have grown stronger and become more comprehensive medical service centers. The Howard University Hospital, in Washington, DC and the Homer G. Phillips Hospital in St. Louis, Missouri are exemplary. These hospitals withstood the changes in laws and the new competition ushered in by desegregation by making improvements in their technological infrastructures, cutting costs, raising salaries to levels competitive with other hospitals and adding other accoutrements.

Racial desegregation of hospitals like public and private schools and other institutions has also meant increased competition with comparable agencies to recruit new members, including staff and well-insured patients among consumers in the marketplace. In chapter 7, on "Doctor Shopping Behavior," we will see a variety of examples of how patients and physicians searched within the health services industries for the best possible outcomes, each in his or her own self-interest. Also discussed are some of the risks of economic losses to which hospitals, physicians, and patients were exposed in the marketplace.

A new challenge to the surviving historically black hospitals and physicians in private practice with large numbers of patients listed among the poor and under-insured has been the rise of managed-care programs. It is difficult to pinpoint the inception of managed-care programs. But their growth and importance has been closely associated with the mushrooming costs of health care, on the one hand, and losses of profits among insurers.

Before managed care, health insurance companies were bound by contract to pay the full costs of bills submitted to them by providers for services rendered the insured. The assumption was that in any given group of insured, individual costs would be spread over the group such that the gross revenues from all premiums would permit the company to realize a profit. However, as hospital costs, disability claims, physicians, and specialists costs have increased, while competition for group accounts have kept pressure on insurers to keep their premiums down, their profit shares have plummeted. These were among the background factors that spurred the conceptualization of managed care programs.

With the enabling legislation of the 1970s, managed care, such as health maintenance organizations, have permitted insurers to negotiate with providers, such as hospitals, to offer their services at discounted prices, or for a pre-set number of inpatient days, and pre-planned limits on other costs in exchange for being selected as a provider of health care under the program of services managed by the insurer. In this kind of arrangement, the provider that could afford to negotiate and offer favorable prices to insurers contributed to his/her own economic security. The problem for many historically black hospitals that were already economically marginal (before the inception of managed care programs), and black physicians with large numbers of poor patients, was their inability to offer competitive discounts to insurers. As a consequence, they have been increasingly squeezed out of the market, already pressured as they were by the other political and economic shifts associated with desegregation in the United States.

We have already discussed various mid-twentieth century changes in laws, public policy, and philanthropic support that foretold the demise of selected black owned and operated hospitals. Among the health care industries major structural shifts were induced by the Supreme Court decision of 1954 in *Brown v. Board of Education of Topeka, Kansas* and the 1965 revisions of the Hill-Burton Hospital Construction Act. More will be said about the legal and social repercussions of these changes as this study unfolds. As movements toward desegregation continue, other domains of health service agencies previously protected and/or sustained, albeit inadvertently, by the closed social relations that racial segregation represented will be challenged to become more competitive in what appears to be an increasingly open society.

Conclusions

Hospitals have been crucial institutions in the long historical struggle of African Americans to achieve specializations in medicine and delivery of comprehensive health care services for their patients. This chapter shows that there were small successes in African American developments of hospitals during the antebellum period. Following the Civil War, however, and the founding of the Freedmen's Bureau, the development of black owned and operated hospitals began to proliferate, especially, but not exclusively in the Southern United States.

By the time of the *Plessy v. Ferguson* decision of 1896, ten programs of medical education for blacks had been established in four Southern states and the District of Columbia. In addition, hundreds of physicians had graduated from those institutions and begun medical practices through which they increasingly saw the need for hospitals to which their patients could be admitted. Constrained in their practices by racial separatism that was partly expressed through segregated health care facilities, these African American physicians and allied health care practitioners had little choice but to develop their own hospitals to facilitate achieving the clinical competencies and service delivery outcomes they sought.

To compensate for the Supreme Court decision of 1896 that set in motion a sixty-year period of juridically sanctioned racial separatism and intensified discrimination against blacks, there began a proliferation of hospitals, nurses training schools, life and health insurance companies, and other agencies favorable to comprehensive health care for blacks. These developments were partly responses to "the mother of invention": cut off from other avenues by which medical specialties could be achieved and programs of comprehensive health care for blacks developed and implemented, there was little choice but that these practitioners construct and operate their own facilities. These were among the major factors helping to account for the rise of hospitals documented in this chapter.

With the 1954 Supreme Court reversal of *Plessy v. Ferguson* and the 1965 amendments to the Hill-Burton Hospital Construction Act, some of the major incentives for black owned and operated hospitals were removed. Corresponding to the twenty-year period (1946–1965) over which these changes occurred, there was a rapid decline in black hospitals. Today, most of the black hospitals of the period of separatism have closed. Managed care programs foretell new competitive pressures to which the few remaining historically black hospitals and other providers must respond. The long-term repercussions of managed care must await future observation and analyses.

This concludes part 1 of our study of the profession of medicine by African American physicians. The focus was on medical education, gender differences in the development of careers and the importance of hospitals as settings that facilitated the practice of medicine. This background helps to set the stage for the analyses of the experiences of black physicians and doctor-patient relations described in part 2.

Notes

1. Aubre de L. Maynard, *A Gallery of Negro Surgeons,* volumes 1 and 2, pp. 113–114 (unpublished and undated). This document was made available through Mrs. Florence Borders, Archivist, The Amistead Research Center, New Orleans, Louisiana, November 21–23, 1985.
2. George Thomas (M.D.)., professional history Interview, New Orleans, Louisiana, August, 1986, p. 37.
3. Darlene Clark Hine, "Health and the Afro-American Family" in *Health* (Washington, DC, The Associated Publishers, 1984), p. 2.
4. Maynard, *A Gallery of Negro Surgeons.*
5. Gunnar Myrdal, *An American Dilemma: The Negro Problem and Modern Democracy* (New Brunswick, NJ: Transaction Publishers, 1996), p. 304.
6. Nathaniel Wesley, Jr., "Searching for Survival: Black Hospitals Listing and Selected Commentary" (Washington, DC: Howard University, School of Business Administration, January 1983).
7. Veterans Administration Medical Center, "In Observance of Black History Month, 1981" (Tuskegee, AL: VMAC, February 1981).
8. William A. Cleland (M.D.), professional history interview, Durham, North Carolina, 1986), p.1.
9. Ibid., p. 2.
10. Ibid., pp. 2–3.
11. Maynard, *A Gallery of Negro Surgeons.*
12. Hubert A. Eaton (M.D.), professional history interview, Wilmington, North Carolina, 1 May 1986.
13. M.C. Hill and B.C. McCall, "Cracker Culture: A Preliminary Definition," *Phylon*, vol. 11, no. 3 (1950), pp. 223–231.
14. Charles Watts (M.D.), professional history interview, Durham, North Carolina, 1986), p.1.
15. Ibid., p. 8.
16. Veterans Administration Medical Center, "In Observance of Black History Month."
17. Ibid., p. 8.
18. Howard Kenney (M.D.), professional history interviews, Tuskegee, Alabama, Spring 1986.

19. Maynard, *A Gallery of Negro Surgeons*, pp. 293–294.
20. "The John A. Andrew Memorial Hospital and Nurse Training School," Archive, Booker T. Washington collection, Main Library (Tuskegee Institute, Alabama, 1993).
21. John A. Andrew Memorial Hospital Cares. Tuskegee Institute Endnotes, chapter 4 (Alabama: Tuskegee Institute, 1975), p. 2. This document is also available in the Booker T. Washington Collection, Tuskegee University, 18 May 1989.
22. Kenney, professional history interview.
23. Fannie Jenkins, School of Nursing and Allied Health, Historical Documents and Interview (Tuskegee University, Tuskegee, Alabama, July 1993).
24. Ibid., interview.
25. Ibid., interview.
26. Ibid., interview.

Part 2

Microstructures of the Social Organization of Health-Care Delivery in the Everyday Life of a Racially Segmented Society

Introduction to Part 2

The special focus of the next four chapters is on black physicians and patients: The variety of obstacles that black patients often faced as help-seekers; that black physicians encountered as help givers; and the differing occasions of face-to-face interaction in which these potential partners came together but sometimes failed to achieve the health care goals that were reasonable to expect between them. The analyses reveals schisms induced by the color line, and occasionally class differences pervasively entrenched in the social structure of interaction, often deeply internalized in the psychological being of the actors, doctors and patients alike, black and white. Many insights are developed through analyses of first-hand accounts told by black physicians of the period.

Chapter 5 addresses selected social and economic constraints on help-seeking behavior. As previous studies have shown, there is not necessarily a straight line trajectory between a person's expression of symptoms of illness and access to health care services. The ability to meet the terms of insurance companies such as Preferred Provider Organizations (PPOs) and Health Maintenance Organizations (HMOs) and the individual health care provider, one doctor's willingness to accept a referral from another, and a variety of other factors help to shape the path of each patient's help-seeking and help-getting behavior.

Chapter 6 continues the discussion of structural factors that shape help-seeking behavior, but focuses in particular on rules against "race mixing," or integration, in the social organization of access to agencies designed to deliver health services. The analyses reveal patterns of segregated times, places, sitting locations, staff-patient interactions and other ways in which attitudes and beliefs about race differences in the United States have helped to determine access to health care services.

Each chapter shows that both doctor and patient are co-participants in a relatively open market: each can, to some extent, and does shop for and select interaction partners from the membership group of the other. While there is no pretense that the patient is an equal partner in the doctor-patient relationship, he or she often exercises selectivity in doctor shopping that can influence the conduct of the physician, as well as the physcian's self-image in the practice of medicine.

Chapter 7 addresses a variety of social, cultural, demographic, and social psychological factors related to the process by which a doctor is selected as a health care provider. Beginning with the assumption of a search for a physician, attention is then turned to the myriad factors that may intervene to guide the prospective patient in one direction or another, culminating in a doctor-patient relationship. In the overall process of seeking help to cope with or prevent illness, it is recognized that the prospective patient may or may not select (or have selected for him/her) a physician. An alternative health care provider, such as a granny midwife versus an obstetrician may be chosen. Although somewhat peripheral to the central focus of this study, chapter 10 develops a discussion of the interfaces of practitioners of "traditional" and biomedicine with implications for alternative approaches to health care.

Finally, chapter 8 discusses processes of sustaining positive self-imagery and a sense of public worth among physicians who happen-to-be black. Through in-depth interviews with older physicians, an attempt is made to unravel differential techniques of coping with the stigma of black identity. Among them were positive psychological, emotional, and social responses to risks of stigma and actual degradation ceremonies. Included are descriptions of characteristics of selected physicians who persisted and achieved some measures of success in the practice of medicine in spite of their unpleasant experiences in the racially stratified society in which they lived.

5

Illness and Economic Constraints on Help-Seeking Behavior

It is bad enough that a man should be ignorant, for this cuts him off from the commerce of men's minds. It is perhaps worse that a man should be poor, for this condemns him to a life of stint and scheming, and there is no time for dreams and no respite from weariness. But what surely is worse is that a man should be unwell, for this prevents him from doing anything much about his poverty or his ignorance.
—Kimball (1970)[1]

Illness is a great leveler of what might otherwise be distinguished, able-bodied, and mentally healthy individuals in the everyday life of society. At one time or another during the life course, everyone experiences some kind and degree of illness, and/or pain whether mild or severe, acute or chronic. Regardless of economic class or race, the physical and/or psychological disorder will have similar individual effects. To some extent, energy will be diminished, lethargy induced, and biological and/or social psychological processes of adaptation set in motion to return the individual to a state of well-being. Among the factors that mediate those effects, however, are the means and manners of individual and group adaptation. It is the adaptive process(es) more than any other factors that account for social and personal coping with illness and subsequent successes in health maintenance.

Economic, Social, and Psychological Facilitators of Adaptation

Possession of the economic means to meet the costs of health care is crucial to individual and group adaptation to illness. Whether the economic means are comprised of income from gainful employment, indirect income, such as health insurance, or bartering for services through the uses of agricultural and other material or personal goods and services, economic factors play major parts in the acquisition of health services.

In some cases, personal economic resources may have been too meager to pay the full costs of health care. On the other hand, there may have been professional discrimination against the poor when, for example, a physician was unwilling to handle claims of Medicaid patients because of low cost-to-reimbursement ratios. There were also health professionals in private practice who restricted treatment of the poor, such as Medicaid patients, to certain days and hours to avoid commingling between them and fee-for-service patients. This kind of practice showed up in private offices, public health clinics and hospital wards. Under these circumstances, the highly motivated poor patient who was determined to achieve or sustain healthy living risked being denied health care or discouraged from sustained attempts to acquire care in spite of his or her good intentions.

Secondly, unpaid family members, friends, church leaders, and members of congregations were often reported among those on the front lines of support groups for individuals in times of illness, especially, but not exclusively for the poor.[2] It is true that the higher the income level, the more options the patient had, and the less likely he/she needed to consider informal and/or unpaid sources of intervention on occasions of illness.[3] It does not follow, however, that the uses of informal sources of health care and social support, such as family members and friends, were strictly a practice of the poor.[4] Other research has shown the cross-class significance of informal support groups as agents of intervention in response to illness.[5] More will be said about this later.

Finally, strong individual motivation to sustain a healthful state of being and avoid debilitating illness may also contribute significantly to coping with illness producing stressors. These behaviors may be expressed through deliberate solicitation of help from informal support groups, or by seeking a therapeutic relationship outside familiar family and neighborhood circles, such as traditional healers.[6]

In the pages that follow, we will describe and discuss concrete illustrations of the bearing of economic structures, primary groups, and individual motivation in the organization of help-seeking behavior. We begin with economic constraints.

Economic Constraints on Intervention Systems

Discrimination and segregation on the basis of race in doctor's waiting rooms was clear, as will be shown in chapter 7. An unanticipated finding, however, reported by two physicians in New Orleans was evidence of discrimination on the basis of class differences among patients.[7] Reported by these physicians were (1) black and white doctors who separated patients by days for office visits on the basis of fee-for-service versus Medicaid as a means of pay, and (2) fee-for-service patients who either did not want to share entire waiting rooms, or sit in the same subsection of a waiting room with the poor.

> Hospitals faced this problem as well as physicians. Somebody comes in there [a hospital or a doctor's waiting room] who's able to afford any kind of medicine,... and here come a Medicaid patient out of the projects across the street, unlearned and unclean.... You got to recognize that when people get to a state in life, they want certain standards maintained.[8]

Some doctors have adapted to consumer concerns about class differences as follows:

> Well, alright, I'll take Medicare and Medicaid patients, and segregate them so they won't have to come and sit up beside somebody that hadn't had a bath in six weeks and that's talking all kinds of dirty language, etc.[9]

As shown in other studies of race relations and economic inequality in the United States, being black and a member of the lower socioeconomic class are two attributes that have a high likelihood of co-varying in the profile of the same individual.[10] A part of the irony and, perhaps the agony for some black physicians was the nearly unalterable claim made upon their services by large numbers of poor and black patients in spite of the physicians preference for fee-for-service patients. Many black physicians who were also entrapped by the color line which constrained most prospective white patients from using their services had little choice except to accept black patients, poor or not, as clientele.

Bartering with the Poor in Exchange for Health Care

Commodity exchange was one alternative to rejecting the poor who could not afford the fee for a given service, and who did not have health insurance. Bartering, for example, the treatment of pneumonia by a physician in exchange for two bushels of apples was common in some localities. The following anecdote depicts the experiences of a black physician in Monticello, Georgia whose proportion of poor patients grew to such large numbers that he required a barn to receive and store the large volumes of commodities due from his economically poor patients.

> I bought a barn out in the country and had it torn down and hauled to my house and put on the back of the lot. This was done so that farmers who owed me could drive into the barn, open their truck or wagon door, and throw off thirty or fifty bushels of corn, or whatever was necessary to pay the doctor.[11]

This physician went on to point out that a large number of physicians whom he knew had similar experiences: "If patients did not have the money," it was not unusual to accept commodities or services in exchange for the doctor's care.

All physicians, however, did not capitulate to demands to serve the poor. Some refused to accept poor patients on any terms. These physicians took the risk of losing future referrals from other physicians whose patients needed specialized treatment, and in some instances, they risked damaging the solvency of their entire private practice in a given locality. Wanting on the one hand to sustain a private practice but not accept patients who were poor could induce a double bind phenomenon.

A double bind is created by dual and conflicting messages that express different intentions of an individual toward the same object. For example, the physician who opens a private practice, presumably to serve anyone with an illness but seeks to exclude the poor sends out conflicting messages. In terms of Bateson's original formulation developed to attempt to account for interpersonal factors that contribute to the development of schizophrenia, the following illustration is useful:

> In many families, communication between members is so confusing that the child may be torn between conflicting feelings and demands. For example, the mother may tell him he is getting too fat, yet offer him sweets as a reward for good behavior; or she may complain that he is not affectionate, yet freeze up when he tries to put his arm around her.[12]

The special focus of this discussion was on physicians who publicly identified as health professionals sworn to uphold the Hippocratic oath, yet attempted to discriminate among patients on the basis of wealth. Ethically, it seems justifiable that licensed physicians should accept an obligation to treat a patient in need of a physician's care, in spite of the patient's economic means (or lack, thereof) to pay the doctor's fee. In addition to risking an offense against a colleague and violating medical ethics, the physician who rejects the poor risks cutting himself/herself off from future referrals of fee-for-service patients. One physician in New Orleans put it this way:

> There are some physicians who wouldn't take referrals of Medicaid or poor patients and got squeezed out, especially in specialized areas, like neurology; they stopped getting any referrals at all. To a certain extent, you got to take what the doctor sends you.... If he's sending you his good patients, then you gotta take some bad ones too.[13]

Discussion

The broad focus of this chapter was on the influence of economic factors on doctor-patient relationships. Special attention was focused on physician attitudes toward the poor and the consequences of their attitudes for health behavior. Health behavior is comprised of a variety of acts, including, but not limited to, those aimed at securing regular medical check-ups to sustain health and/or to prevent illness from occurring. Help seeking can be an extension of either illness or health behavior that is manifest in response to a real or anticipated disorder for which intervention is needed. Chapter 6, on "race in the structure of access to treatment," shows how the racial identity of the prospective patient and health care provider may interact, in some instances, to constrain the consumption of health care services even though the patient may have the economic means to achieve that end.

Notes

1. G.H. Kimball, "Twentieth Century Fund," in *The Biennial Report* (North Carolina Board of Health, 1968–70), p. 55.
2. Wilbur H. Watson, *Aging and Social Behavior: An Introduction to Social Gerontology* (CA: Wadswoth, 1982); also see Sarah E. Rix and Tania Romashko. *With a Little Help from My Friends* (Washington, DC: American Institute for Research, 1980).
3. Wilbur H. Watson, *Black Folk Medicine: The Therapeutic Significance of Faith and Trust* (New Brunswick, NJ: Transaction Publishers, 1984).
4. Watson, *Aging and Social Behavior.*
5. Talcott Parsons, "Social Structure and Dynamic Process: The Case of Modern Medical Practice," pp. 428–479 in *The Social System*, by Talcott Parsons (New York: The Free Press, 1951); also see E. Gartley Jaco (ed.), *Doctors, Patients and Illness: A Source Book in Behavioral Science and Health* (New York: The Free Press, 1972).
6. Watson, *Black Folk Medicine.*
7. George Thomas (M.D.), professional history interview, New Orleans, Louisiana, 1986, p. 46; see also C.C. Haydell (M.D.), professional history interview, New Orleans, Louisiana, 1986.

8. Thomas, p. 42.
9. Ibid, p. 43.
10. John C. Norman (ed.), *Medicine in the Ghetto* (New York: Appleton-Century-Crofts, 1969). See also William Julius Wilson, *The Truly Disadvantaged* (Chicago: University of Chicago Press, 1987); and Douglas S. Massey and Nancy A. Denton, *American Apartheid* (Cambridge, MA: Harvard University Press, 1993).
11. Frederick Funderburg (M.D.), professional history interview, Atlanta, Georgia, 1985, p. 15.
12. Gregory Bateson, "Minimal Requirements for a Theory of Schizophrenia." *Archives of General Psychiatry* vol. 2 (1960), pp. 477–91; Also see Robert M. Goldenson, *The Encyclopedia of Human Behavior*, vol. 2 (New York: Doubleday and Company, 1970), pp. 1162–1163.
13. Thomas, p. 44.

6

Race in the Structure of Access to Treatment

*Pain and desire for its relief are the basic motives of
the patient, and they are diminished by any of the
elements of contradiction in the doctor-patient
relationship. The prospective patient will not stop
seeking help, but the way these dilemmas are
managed will figure in what he seeks help for; whom
he seeks help from; and how he will behave in
consultation. How some of the dilemmas are managed, of course, also involves the physician; his
willingness and ability to accommodate to the patient,
and the presence of situations in which he must
accommodate if he is to keep his practice. They are
reflected in the way he tries to deal with the patient.
Thus, the doctor-patient relationship is not a
constant, but obviously a variable.*
— Fredison (1962)[1]

In the foreword to *Medicine in the Ghetto*,[2] Norman and Bennett
point out that many citizens in the United States are "denied the full
benefits of medical science because they are poor and because they are
confined by social, economic and cultural forces to isolation in the ghettoes of our large urban centers." While this is an accurate observation,
with broad examples given throughout *Medicine in the Ghetto*, the historical and social psychological depth of the problem of segregation by
race within the practice of medicine is not fully demonstrated. In addition to developing insight into the problem of access to health services
by inhabitants of black ghettoes, focusing in particular on the period
from 1896 to 1965, this chapter presents microsociological illustrations and analyses of race and social interaction within the contexts of
segregated wards, waiting rooms, and other facilities designed for the
delivery of health care services.

Race-related structures of oppressive dominance were legion during the period of the "nadir" in the United States and lingered at least through the mid-twentieth century. Rayford W. Logan defined the nadir as the lowest point in the quest for equal rights in the history of the United States,[3] beginning in the 1870s.

One would have thought that the humanistic intentions of the health care professions would have compelled the exemption of hospitals and medical clinics from the effects of racism seen elsewhere in society. But that was not the case in the practice of medicine in the United States.

We will show that in some instances during the period of separatism, it was not sufficient for a black patient to have economic means and high social status when seeking health care. Nor did membership in the medical profession necessarily make a difference when a black person decided to seek medical care from a white physician or an institutional agency. The multifaceted structural constraints that operated on many occasions to frustrate the selection of a particular physician will be discussed in detail in the next chapter. In the following pages of this chapter, however, we will show that the risk of dehumanizing treatment for many black patients began in earnest after entering the domain of the doctor's office.

Our findings show patterns of segregation in: (1) pathways to and from health care facilities; (2) days of the week, and times of day when a black person could see a doctor; (3) sitting locations in doctors' waiting rooms; (4) hospital wards; and (5) staffing patterns among allied health professionals in hospitals and outpatient clinics. In the following discussion, we will describe and interpret each of these expressions of segregation in the social organization of health care.

Queuing for Access: Entering and Exiting Health Care Facilities

Hardly any domain of social life where blacks and whites came in contact was spared the regulatory tentacles of racial separatism. Points of access to and egress from public buildings, such as racially mixed hospitals, were no exception.

Queuing is the practice of lining up and waiting to receive a service, such as paying for goods purchased in a supermarket, or waiting for a teller in a bank to cash a check. Blacks waiting for medical services in racially mixed gatherings often experienced the intrusion of the color line in that process. The following anecdote illustrates this problem as described by a black physician affiliated with a small predominantly white hospital in Monticello, Georgia during the 1940s.

There was a small group of beds for black patients near the rear of the hospital and it was the custom that black patients and staff enter through the back door.

> [The hospital] was shared by blacks and whites. I went in the back door as was my custom at that time. All the Negroes went in from back there. I [the only black physician in town] went back there with them [the black patients] as a protest against them having to go there.[4]

In this anecdote, the only black physician in town was permitted to enter the hospital by the front or back door, but treated his patients in the back wards to which they were restricted. His egress through the back door, as told in the anecdote, was intended by him as a symbolic protest, rather than full compliance with the racially separatist customs of the times.

Sacred and Profane Periods of Time

Some white doctors achieved segregation of blacks from whites by designating times rather than places, such as days of the week for blacks that were distinguished from the days allocated to whites. In addition to the spatial separation of blacks and whites, they were temporally and visually separated from each other. In some doctors' offices, neither white nor black patients saw each other at the same time in the same place. The following quote is illustrative:

> There are some [white doctors] here [in Shreveport] who have a day for blacks, which is Wednesday. They arrange it. They don't see the white woman. I wouldn't have known that until the medical school sent me a young girl as an externship to spend six weeks in the summer to study under me. I examined her one day. She had endometriosis. And I called a [white] colleague to see her. He said, "yes," I will see her on Wednesday at such-and-such a time." So, when the girl came back to me she said, "Are you aware that I didn't see one white patient there, and I am a native of Shreveport. I want you to investigate that thing." You see how naive I was. I went to investigate it. And he [the white doctor] had the courage to tell me that "the blacks want it that way, and the whites want it that way."[5]

The depth of the institutionalization of the color line in the separation of blacks from whites showed no respect for class or status differences among blacks. Even black physicians, for example, were restricted from seeing white colleagues in medicine on days set aside for whites only. The following passage is illustrative:

I had a child that had a fracture of the wrist, and a [white] medical colleague was treating the child for me. And he wanted to talk to me. So, he told me to come to the orthopedic clinic which happened to be on a day for whites, so that we could talk about it. So, I went there, and the clinic door was closed. And of course, I knocked on the door of the entrance to the clinic, and the white nurse came to the door. She said, "you're going to have to come back later, this ain't Negro day". And so, I told her, "well [the doctor] called me and told me to come by here so he could talk to me." So she went over there and told him that "a nigger was out here" who said he wanted to talk to him. I had given her my name. He said, "look, if you want to continue to work here, if a black *bear* comes out there and asks for me, you better let him in."[6]

It should be noted that the segregation of waiting rooms was not merely a consequence of doctor decision making. The values and beliefs about the importance of racial separation were pervasive. The following anecdote shows the bearing of patient values and influences on separatism. In this instance, it was a black patient who objected to white patients coming to a black physician for treatment.

The second year I was here, some white patients came to see me. The black in the waiting room objected to that. I remember that very well. She said, "I want you to do me a favor. There are two whites in the waiting room, waiting to see you. I will pay the $5.00, that's $10.00 for the two, but I want you to have the courage to tell them that you do not treat whites." I said, "Mrs. B., it's a violation of my ethics. I was trained to preserve life. They never mentioned white or black. I cannot tell those people that. If those people want to see me, I am going to see them." I ended up seeing them, and I ended up seeing the black who complained but the white people did not return.[7]

Segregated Waiting Rooms and Private Practices

Getting an appointment for medical care is a beginning, but not sufficient to consummate access to a physician. If the physician was white and the patient was black in the United States between 1896 and 1965, the patient also had to maneuver his/her way through the race-related social structure of the doctor's waiting room, if it was a private practice, or the hospital service system, if it was institutional:

In practically every office you went into we had segregated waiting rooms. You might get there at eight o'clock in the morning, but if you were black, in many instances you would be the last patient to be seen. As long as the whites were there, it was just like getting on the bus, you know. The bus could be empty, but you gotta go sit in the back.[8]

The roots of the rules for racial segregation illustrated by this passage can be traced to historical patterns of discrimination against blacks.

Over the decades of oppression, many black physicians adjusted their practices to comply with these customs. In the following anecdote that illustrates an instance of capitulation to custom, the black physician goes one step further by discouraging white patients entirely from coming to him for treatment. His intent, however, was not merely to discriminate against whites, but to try to minimize the waiting room adjustments required of his black patients by excluding whites as interaction partners.

> I had both [black and white patients], but I discouraged the whites as much as I could. For example, one day I was in the office and came into the waiting room, and a white mother came in there with her child. One of my black mothers got up to give her a seat. That shows you how they thought. I tried to provide them with a decent place because at that time when they [blacks] went to the white doctor's office, they went to basement areas, side doors or other areas.[9]

A more pointed example of the social and psychological dynamics of racial segregation and the fear and expected consequences of violating customary race relations is illustrated in the following quotation from a physician in North Carolina:

> One day, a patient who had been coming here [to my private office] for years, saw three white patients out there [in the waiting room]. When she got in [for treatment], she said, "you goin let them folks run us out of here doc?" She was upset. It just happened that day that there were three [white patients] who were referred from the emergency room [of Durham County Hospital] to an outpatient clinic. They had been to the emergency room, been sewed up, and it was my turn to take calls; so they made these appointments for me.[10]

The black patient's concern was that the "cake of custom" had been violated, and that the white folks might decide to conscript the offices of the black physician for their exclusive use.

One doctor interviewed for this study in Shreveport, Louisiana pointed out that "there are a few white doctors who started their practices in the 1950s with dual [black and white] waiting rooms and are still practicing [medicine] in Shreveport."[11] He hastened to add that their repugnant perspectives on blacks have not changed, only the circumstances, primarily the laws.

Another example of racial segregation in the social organization of sitting locations is provided by an older black physician in Durham, North Carolina:

> One day I was eating my evening meal, and a black mother called me quite anxiously and wanted to know if I could come back to the office to see her child. She

said the bus would leave soon, and that would be the last chance she would have to get back home. So, I told her I would see her, although she was not a patient of mine. When I got to the office, she started cursing. She said, "I'm not cursing you; I'm cursing that [other doctor]. I came over here this morning, and I've been down there in his room [basement] all this time waiting for him to see my child. And he called me up after he had seen all the white patients, and another white mother came in, and he left me to see her." She was angry. She had been waiting down in the furnace room. That's where he had his black patients wait.[12]

In the immediately foregoing examples, the waiting rooms for white patients were upstairs and the waiting rooms for black patients were in the basements of each white doctor's office. Variations on these patterns of racial stratification and segregation of places are replete throughout the professional historical interviews carried out during this study.

Ghetto Hospitals and Wards

In hospitals primarily designed to serve the interests of whites, like the waiting rooms of white physicians, blacks were segregated by means of access, spatial allocation, and quality of care. A microcosm of the practice is illustrated by an excerpt from an interview with an elderly physician in Durham, North Carolina.

I think from the very beginning, they had one ward where all the black patients were placed regardless of their illness, except obstetrics. [Black] obstetrical patients were handled in a manner different from white ones. They stayed overnight; sometimes they didn't stay the full day. They were delivered on stretchers and sent on back home. They were doing this before other hospitals started during the [Second World] War period. Duke just started in 1930. They expanded the [Duke University] hospital just before the War. But when the War started and they couldn't do any further expansion, having outgrown the facilities, they curtailed any services for black obstetrical patients, except most of the local ones who were delivered at Lincoln [a local hospital set aside for blacks]. But people would come from surrounding areas to be delivered. They had O.B. clinic and they had a fee for teaching purposes, so they would deliver black women and send them home. This caused a little problem because we frequently had to readmit them at Lincoln if they had complications. They never did that for whites. They had this program for black women, but not for whites.[13]

Even though obstetrical services were rendered black patients, there was race-related discrimination in the quality of care. For example:

When white patients were admitted, they stayed five to seven days [on the average]. Between the years 1930 and 1940, the state of the art was fourteen days. If you had a baby, and you were white, you could expect to have a hospital bed for up to two weeks.... [Whites] got the normal treatment. Black women went home the same day.[14]

In the following passage, another physician provides another illustration of the poor quality of hospital care for black patients. In this instance, the beds for blacks are both segregated and located in a separate building, disconnected from the main building, including operation rooms of the hospital.

> They had wards for blacks. Here, it was kind of bad. They had a special section; special buildings for blacks. When they had to do an operation, the operating room was in the main section of the building, and the wards were detached. Sometimes they had to roll them [black patients] out through the weather, back and forth. I read somewhere that they do the same thing up in West Virginia. This was the bastion of medical practice in this area. It was controlled by whites. Black doctors couldn't go there [into the main building]. Black doctors had no privileges whatsoever.[15]

White Hands Can Do No Harm

"Laying on of hands" is an expression often heard in reference to the internship experiences of physicians, nurses, and other health and allied health professionals. There is a small literature on sex codes for nurses in bedside manners with male patients, but little is reported on race codes for physicians, nurses, or other staff.[16] Reports of several informants, however, that developed through this research provided some insights into customs of the period of separatism suggesting rules that regulated contact across the color line in hospitals. A retired physician in New Orleans described the differential rights of white and black physicians as follows:

> We had two different hospitals. They [white physicians] kept the regular city hospital they had all the time; they just segregated the wards. When they built Reynolds Memorial Hospital, it was a separate building all together with nothing but blacks in it. White doctors rotated their house staff through both hospitals, white and black. But black doctors rotated in the hospital for blacks, only.[17]

Here is demonstrated yet another expression of the socially unequal relations between blacks and whites. While both groups of physician's had been fully trained by some of the best medical schools in the country and licensed to practice medicine in Louisiana, blacks were constrained from observing and treating white patients, while white physicians had the liberty to observe and treat or not treat whomever they wished. This kind of discrimination was not peculiar to southern Louisiana. Nor has it fully disappeared since desegregation, 1965. While its expression has waned, as one black surgeon in Monroe suggests, some white doctors still frown upon black surgeons operating on white patients.

> Any time I operated on a white patient, I could see that the white doctors did not like it. But now [in 1986], [white objections] are subtle.[18]

While most black hospitals were preponderantly staffed by black physician's and nurses, mobility of nurses between black and white hospitals and patient care between them was less constrained than the mobility of their physician counterparts. Perhaps black nurses in contrast to black physicians were perceived as less threatening, or less likely to befoul white staff and patients should contact occur.

Less surprising was the inequality between blacks and whites, doctors and nurses, in their assignments to positions of rank in hospital hierarchies of authority.

> Most of the whites were supervisors of staff. Most of the people who were actually doing work were blacks. Most black hospital workers were aides, not registered nurses. They just weren't at the top.[19]

Conclusions

This chapter documents racial ghettoes within the health and medical establishment of the United States. Moreover, it shows the extent to which race-related social oppression can innervate the life of a society and shape the values, beliefs, and rules for social interaction even in the care of the sick. But, as tragic and incredible as some of these portrayals were, the responses of many blacks were proactive, with a strong determination to find ways to improve the health and life chances of blacks and other patients for whom black physicians were responsible.

We turn next to a discussion of doctor shopping, a process closely related to access. Here we address the multifaceted factors that influence patient decision making, especially African Americans, in selecting a doctor. As we will show, racial parity between patient and physician, and intensity of need for health care were often less compelling than patient prejudices and other factors that helped to shape social perceptions and choices of physicians.

Notes

1. Eliot Freidson, "Dilemmas in the Doctor Patient Relationship," p. 222 in Arnold M. Rose (ed.), *Human Behavior and Social Processes: An Interactionist Approach* (Boston: Houghton Mifflin Company, 1962).

2. John C. Norman and Beverly Bennett, "Foreword," pp. xxi–xxii in John C. Norman (ed.), *Medicine in the Ghetto* (New York: Appleton-Century-Crofts, 1969), p. xxi.
3. Rayford W. Logan, *The Betrayal of the Negro* (London: Collier Books, 1965), p. 11.
4. Fred Funderburg (M.D.), professional history interview, Atlanta, Georgia, 1985, p. 5.
5. Jean Breire (M.D.), professional history interview, Shreveport, Louisiana, Feb. 1986, p. 24.
6. William Alexander Cleland (M.D.), professional history interview, Durham, North Carolina, Aug. 1986, p. 11.
7. Breire, pp. 25–26.
8. George Thomas (M.D.), professional history interview, New Orleans, Louisiana, 1986, p. 41.
9. Cleland, p. 6.
10. Charles Watts, (M.D.), professional history interview, Durham, North Carolina, Mar. 28, 1986, pp. 33–34.
11. Breire, p. 24.
12. Cleland, p. 7.
13. Watts, p. 5.
14. Ibid., p. 6.
15. Leroy Upperman (M.D.), professional history interview, Wilmington, North Carolina, 2 May 1986, pp. 7–8.
16. Wilbur H. Watson and Robert Maxwell, *Human Aging and Dying: A Study In Sociocultural Gerontology* (New York: St. Martins Press, 1977, see part 2); see also Wilbur H. Watson (1976), "Touching Behavior: Geriatric Nursing." *J. Communication* 25 (3):101–112.
17. Thomas, p. 2.
18. Breire, p. 25.
19. Thomas, p. 3.

7

Doctor Shopping Behavior

*Doctor shopping by black patients who raise race
into bold relief as a raison d'être for selecting one
doctor over another is a striking modern day example
of the social, economic, and psychological
consequences of a peoples' internalization
of their oppressor.*
—Watson (1986)[1]

Previous research on doctor shopping is meager. Of the few studies reported in the literature, most have focused on factors related to patient satisfaction and dissatisfaction with medical care; attitudes toward physicians, and patients' choices of physicians for second opinions on prescribed care. The influence of confidence, or lack thereof, in the physician on patient compliance with the prescribed medical regimen is also an important topic in this area of study.[2] Fewer studies have focused on structural factors in the context of shopping, such as long waits, high fees, and distance between the patient's home and the doctor's office.[3] There has been even less research on social and cultural factors, such as race, class, sex, and education at the interfaces of patient-doctor relationships, and the negotiation of service consumption once a patient selects, or is selected by a physician. This analysis focuses on the latter subset of research questions.

Demographic Influences on Choice

Racial separatism and discrimination against blacks, forces that were institutionally prevalent in the United States during the early twentieth century, suggest that it would be reasonable to expect choices of white doctors by white patients, and black doctors by black patients. However, although small by proportion, it was surprising to find that 12 percent of the older whites in this study reported going to black physicians for treatment.[4] For the same reasons that the findings for the majority of older whites were not surprising, the results for older blacks were astounding: 88 percent of older blacks reported going to white physicians when they needed medical services.

My initial hunch was that health care needs in combination with the absence of sufficient numbers of black physicians, or whites for that matter, would (1) compel many patients of the opposite racial group in the local area to seek services across the color line, and (2) the economic return that physicians could expect would compel some to open their doors to patients, black or white, in spite of the color line. The following excerpt from an interview with a black physician in North Carolina helps to corroborate this hunch:

> In some areas of North Carolina, black physicians were the only ones in the county. That was true in parts of Georgia too. In Monticello, Georgia, I made rounds there with [an older black physician] in a little hospital. He had fourteen patients, only two of them were black. He was the best doctor in the county, and the only one in Monticello. In rural areas, black physicians have been treating white folks since the early part of the century.[5]

From this excerpt we can conclude that some selections of black doctors by white patients, and some selections of white doctors by black patients were accounted for by default, especially in rural counties or subareas, thereof, where the shortage of physicians, black or white, precluded selectivity based upon preferences for racial parity between patient and physician. Nevertheless consumer attitudes toward race of the physician must also be taken into account in attempts to understand doctor shopping behavior.

Attitudes and Behavior in Doctor Shopping

A variety of studies in social psychology have shown the high risk of error in attempting to predict behavior from attitudinal expressions.[6] The current study of doctor shopping reported in this chapter corroborates these earlier findings. There were, however, some differences by race in attitudes toward doctor shopping behavior.

When asked about their preferences for a black or a white doctor, provided there was an option, 62 percent of the older whites in this study said that race did not matter, thirty five percent preferred a white doctor, and three percent preferred a black doctor. In response to the same question, 57 percent of the older blacks said race did not matter,

37 percent preferred a black doctor, and six percent preferred a white doctor. The chi-square test of contingency showed that older blacks were not significantly different from whites in their race related preferences for medical doctors.

When we focused on actual consumption, and asked to whom do you usually go when you are sick, there was a significant difference between blacks and whites. As shown in table 7.1, older whites (88 percent) overwhelmingly went to white physicians. That was not surprising. The remaining 12 percent said that they used the services of nonwhite physicians. Older blacks, in surprisingly large numbers, 88 percent, did not use the services of black physicians.

Situational Ethics in the Choice of Black Physicians by White Patients

There were situations in which decision making by white patients in the choice of a black physician were motivated by other than medical interests. For example, there was a number of black physicians who revealed that, in many instances, before 1965, they saw whites who could not afford to pay the fee-for-service at the time that medical care was needed and came to the black physician expecting treatment with a delayed payment plan; an expression of race-related supplication expected of black physicians by some white patients. In other instances, news about the economic generosity of some black physicians was widespread, having become public knowledge among whites as well as blacks. These were physicians who had become known for providing health care without a fee for the poor.[7] The finding of a practice among

TABLE 7.1
Actual Consumption of Medical Services
by Race of Patient and Race of Doctor

Race of Physician	Race of Patient	
	Black	White
Black	12%	12%
White	88%	88%
N(1648)	1521	127
	$x^2= 473.92$, p<.0000, 1df.	

Source: Wilbur H. Watson, "Informal Social Networks in Support of Older Blacks in the Black Belt of the United States," (Washington, DC: The National Center on Black Aged, 1980.)

blacks of waving fees for the poor is consistent with earlier research by Brooks on the effects of high fees-for-services.[8] What is different, however, is the racial crossover by whites. Whether or not poor whites sought generous physicians, regardless of race, during the period of separatism is a question for further research. There were no reported instances, however, in this study.

More frequently reported were instances in which white patients needed a black physician to treat a disorder, such as venereal disease or drug addiction, that the patient wanted concealed from white significant others. By agreeing to intervene, the black physician in effect assisted the white patient in "face saving" among other whites by whom the patient was known, or might then become known following treatment.[9] Goffman defined *face saving* as those acts engaged by an individual or significant others to sustain the positive social value a person effectively claims for himself or herself.[10] Patient decision making aimed at face saving is illustrated by a black physician in New Orleans:

> They [white patients] run out sooner or later in the white community and they figure they can come to me [a black physician] and they may say, well "he's not as apt to catch on to what we're doing." The average white patient that we [black doctors] treat is either a patient who has venereal disease or somebody looking for drugs. A lot of those people are hooked into drugs.... Usually, these are low status people.[11]

By the presence of the color line, that functioned as an effective barrier against referrals and communication between blacks and whites, the patient who saw a black physician for treatment of a deviant disorder, or any other kind, could be reasonably assured that his/her disorder and treatment would not become public among whites. Whether or not the black physician self-consciously decided to conceal his white patient load, the risk of punitive treatment by whites and blacks for violating the color line, led most to keep that information confidential.

Sex and Choice

When sex of the patient was considered in relation to preferences for black or white physicians, the absence of differences between the attitudes of blacks and whites still held. Black and white males, and black and white females were just as likely to express a preference for a physician of their own race as they were likely to say that race did not matter.

Older males and females, however, differed somewhat on reports of actual consumption. Eighty-six percent of the white males reported using

TABLE 7.2
Actual Consumption of Medical Services by Black and White Females

| Race of Physician | Race and Sex of Patient | |
	Black Women	White women
Black	11%	10%
White	89%	90%
N(971)	902	69
	x^2= 276.1,p<.0000, 1df.	

Source: Wilbur H. Watson, "Informal Social Networks in Support of Older Blacks In the Black Belt of the United States," (Washington, DC: The National Center on Black Aged, 1980).

white physicians when sick, and 88 percent of older black males reported using whites (x^2=192.5, p<.0000, Idf).

Both older black and white women, unlike males, showed somewhat stronger biases in their actual consumption of medical services. Surprisingly, black women showed utilization of white physicians in proportions nearly identical to their white counterparts. Ninety percent of the older white women, as shown in table 7.2, reported using white physicians and 89 percent of older black women reported using white physicians.

Class, Status, and Doctor Shopping

A number of factors converged to suggest the importance of socioeconomic class and social status as key factors that help to determine choice. For example, as shown in table 7.3, persons who were unem-

TABLE 7.3
Employment Status and Preferences for Doctors by Race

| Preference for Doctor of like Race | Employment Status | |
	Employed	Unemployed
Yes	54%	36%
No	5%	6%
Does not matter	41%	58%
N(1668)	93	1575
	x^2=11.85, p<.0027, 2df	

Source: Wilbur H. Watson, "Informal Social Networks in Support of Older Blacks In the Black Belt of the United States," (Washington, DC: The National Center on Black Aged, 1980).

ployed were overwhelmingly nondiscriminating in their choices of physicians.

One good reason for this finding is the absence of economic bargaining power: The unemployed, who tend to be highly represented among the poor, lack the economic means to exercise choice, such as Medicaid versus fee-for-service medicine among avenues through which medical services can be secured. Being employed part-time and/or retired had no significant relationship to preferences for a black or white physician.

Considering the owner's estimated value of his/her home as an indicator of economic class, we gained additional insight into class effects on attitudes toward doctor shopping. Among patients for whom racial preference mattered, there was an increasing preference for racial parity between themselves and the physician by whom they were treated as home worth increased from $10,000 to $24,000. Then, among persons with homes valued at more than $24,000. there was a steady decline in the significance assigned to racial parity as home worth approached and exceeded 51,000 or more dollars.

Even more interesting were the results for persons reporting that racial parity did not matter. As the estimated value of a home increased, there were successive decrements in the proportions of those persons who answered that racial parity did not matter. The first finding suggests a curvilinear hypothesis: the higher the level of economic class, up to $24,000, the greater the concern with parity. However, as economic class continues to climb, a decreasing importance is assigned to race of the physician.

The second finding showed an inverse relationship between home worth and preference for racial parity among persons who assigned little or no value to race of the physician. The higher the income, the lower the importance assigned to the color of the physician from whom medical services were sought. Finally, a chi-square test of the effect of education, showed no significant relationship between level of formal education and preferences for racial parity.

Distance of Physicians' Offices from
Low Income and Rural Neighborhoods

Previous research has shown, as we found in this study, that distance between the patient's home and the doctor's office is an important structural obstacle to acquiring medical care.[12] Partly because of rural to urban population migrations, the concern of physicians with securing just remuneration for their services, and the importance of an office location near a medical center, there has been a declining presence of medical doctor's private practices in rural settings since the turn of the century. (See chapter 9 for more detail). For related reasons, low income inner-city neighborhoods also rank low among places likely to be selected for the location of a doctor's office.[13]

Our findings showed that black patients living in predominantly black and rural counties in the South were significantly more likely than their white counterparts to have to travel outside their county of residence for medical care ($X^2=57.44$, p<.0000, 3df). Comparable data on urban settings were not available. While this finding held for black males and females, it was stronger for females. This finding was partly accounted for by the fact that black women went to the doctor more often than black males, and that the specialized services that they needed were most likely to be located outside the rural counties in urban settings near where they lived.

It was not surprising to find that the service providers consulted most often were family medical practitioners. While 68 percent of white males and 73 percent of white females living in the rural South found access to a family medicine physician in their county of residence, only 40 percent of black males and 38 percent of black females secured this kind of medical care in their home counties.

Because of impairment of extremities among many of the patients in this study, physical therapy was a treatment in high demand. While the majority of rural whites, male and female, who needed physical therapy were able to secure this kind of treatment in their county of residence, 46 percent of the black males and 56 percent of the black females had to travel outside their counties of residence for treatment. Comparable problems were not reported in urban settings.

Among consumers of alternative medicine, such as herbal remedies, only black males, and both black and white females reported using these services. Fifty-seven percent of the black males said the office of their alternative medicine service provider was located in their county of residence. Among older black and white women, midwives were the primary sources of alternative medicine. Eighty-six percent of the white woman and 75 percent of the black women said their sources of midwifery were in their counties of residence. The greater presence and accessibility of practitioners of alternative medicine in rural counties in contrast to practitioners of biomedicine, who were more concentrated in urban settings, is consistent with the findings of other studies that document the "vanishing" country doctor (see chapter 9), and the persistence of folk medicine especially, but not exclusively, in the rural pockets of poverty in the United States.[14]

The Importance of Race, Employment and Education

Finally, analysis of variance was performed to determine the combined effects of several different factors on the actual consumption of services from medical doctors. The independent variables considered were race, sex, age (ranging from 60–92 years), education, employment (full-time or not), preference for a doctor who is black or white, home worth, private health insurance, or Medicaid.

Race, employment, and education, in that order, accounted for 74 percent of the variance in actual consumption (see table 7.4). This finding is consistent with the expected effects of racial separatism.

While the separate analyses of home worth and education suggested that those factors might be important in a multivariate analysis of consumption, neither of these factors considered separately were significantly related to actual use of black or white physicians. Similarly, race preference (or attitudes toward black and white physicians), insurance (public or private), were not significantly related to actual consumption of services. Even more subtle than the influences of income, home worth, employment status, and education on the social structure of doctor shopping was the maneuvering shown by some patients in trying to

TABLE 7.4
Results of Multiple Analysis of Variance Controlling For
Race, Employment, and Education

Sum of Squares	df	Mean Square	F	Significance of level	p
Main Effects	73.697	4	18.424	137.596	0.000
Race	66.781	1	66.781	498.735	p<0.000*
Employment	.741	1	0.741	5.535	p<0.019*
Education	.471	2	0.238	1.780	0.169
	73.617	4			

*Effects are significant at the .01 or higher levels of confidence; much greater than what would be expected by chance.

Source: Wilbur H. Watson, "Informal Social Networks in Support of Older Blacks in the Black Belt of the United States," (Washington, DC: The National Center on Black Aged, 1980).

manipulate outcomes in the hospitals to which they were referred and the doctors by whom they were to be treated. The idea of "better sick" patients, which surfaced in one of the field work interviews in North Carolina, illustrated the idea.

"Better Sick" Patients and Status-Seeking Physicians

There are some characteristics of patients, real and idealized, that physicians tend to prize. There may be a variety of attributes of the "better sick," but the primary characteristic is the ability to pay the expected fee for service, with or without insurance. Not only are there characteristics revealed in how the "better sick" discharge their debts, but they show as well in where they go for treatment, showing more selectivity than their less fortunate sick counterparts in choice of doctor and place, such as, the hospital through which treatment is received. In fact, according to one black surgeon in Durham, North Carolina, black physicians showed a kind of selective positioning similar to that observed among patients who wanted to be treated in the best possible hospital environment. Physicians, however, differed from patients in the material goals of their positioning: They wanted to secure residencies and hospital staff positions through which they could expect to reap the greatest gain in training and prestige, as well as improving their economic return through wages and fees-for-services relative to their investments in becoming a physician.

As a consequence of their status-seeking activities, "better sick" patients and capitalistic physicians had similar medical-ecological goals: Becoming housed in the most technologically advanced and economically endowed medical centers. These goals led to frequent convergences or joint participation of these doctors and patients in highly ranked medical centers, such as the Duke University Hospital. The following quotation depicts a scenario in North Carolina:

> Black physicians tended to position themselves to attachment: They came to Durham, Raleigh, Chapel Hill, Greensboro, Winston Salem, and Charlotte. There would be some in between, but for those who were going to practice surgery, or work in hospitals, they would position themselves there [in or around Durham] because that's where the *better sick patients* would go. Black people would go to that area to get their care, 'cause at home they would be put in a basement or not admitted to their hospital at all.[15]

Improvements in the economic means of blacks, such as the acquisition of health insurance has influenced their choices of physicians as well as the perceptions of them (black patients) by white and black physicians and their willingness to accept blacks as patients. This process of selectivity in doctor shopping in association with economic means is illustrated by a black physician in Wilmington, North Carolina:

> Years back when most patients were poor, and school teachers weren't making any money and all that, you would treat the whole family, and take care of all the problems and the ailments and all these things. And most times you wouldn't get paid for it, even with my surgical experience. I can do a hysterectomy. I've done gastrectomies. I've done orthopedic procedures...a whole lot of things; appendectomies, tonsillectomies and all. But when the situations changed where black people started getting insurance coverage and they had insurance policies that would pay them, two things happened: the white physicians accepted them [blacks] more freely, and a lot of them [black patients] abandoned "us" [black physicians]. I say us as a general group. And it used to hurt me when I knew people that I worked with, and I'd hear through the grapevine that they went to some [white] specialist to have a hysterectomy. The least they could have done would be to come and say, "Doctor, I'm thinking about having an operation, and I understand that Dr. so-and-so is a specialist and maybe I'd feel better with him." I'd feel good about this. But when you hear it through the grapevine, it's a hell of a thing.[16]

Securing the services of a physician for purposes of health care is clearly a complex process. More than a mere matter of choice on the part of the prospective patient, it is a negotiated outcome. Although not always a process in which the doctor and patient discussed their conjoint interests, the doctor, like the patient can also be selective and forceful in determining the outcome of shopping behavior: He may decide not to accept the patient, in spite of being the chosen one. Under these circumstances, the patient's search would go on. For many people, not the least of whom were black and/or poor, when confronted with high economic costs and other obstacles to biomedical care, the shopping process sometimes turned inward, culminating in the use of self-prepared home remedies; "healing thyself," as it were. In other instances, patients turned to a traditional medical practitioner or showed a triangular approach to consumption, combining considerations of home remedies, biomedical and traditional medical prescriptions. The interfaces of biomedical and traditional medicine practitioners is discussed in chapter 10.[17]

Conclusions

No matter where black physicians turned in the practice of medicine under separatism, they were exposed to symbols of the color line. Not only did the color line bear upon and shape the practice of medicine externally, it also influenced self-perception and decision making by some black physicians and patients as a consequence of the internalization of the beliefs, values, and rules for behavior of that period. As such, doctor shopping behavior by many blacks revealed their aversion to physicians who happened to be black, so far as that was perceived as an indicator of the character or competence of the doctor considered as a source of health care services. Socially, this meant that a doctor who was perceived as black may be treated as repugnant by some blacks and whites, and often, was only secondarily considered (if at all) as a provider to turn to when health care was needed. But this process was not as simple as these conclusions may suggest. Doctor shopping was (and still is) a multifaceted process, with each facet shaped by race, class and a variety of other factors. While some of these factors were described and empirically examined in this chapter, the significance of the analyses for social policy and further research will be embellished further in the following chapters.

Notes

1. Wilbur H. Watson, *Field Notes and Early Thoughts on Black Physicians and Separatism in the United States* (Atlanta, GA: Center on Health and Aging, Atlanta University, 1986).
2. Milton S. Davis, "Attitudinal and Behavioral Aspects of the Doctor-Patient Relationship as Expressed and Exhibited by Medical Students and Their Mentors," *Journal of Medical Education* vol. 43 (1986), pp. 337–43; Also see Eliot Freidson, "Dilemmas in the Doctor-Patient Relationship," pp. 207–24 in Arnold M. Rose (ed.), *Human Behavior and Social Processes* (Boston: Houghton Mifflin, 1962).
3. Charles H. Brooks, "Associations among Distance, Patient Satisfaction, and Utilization of Two Types of Inner-City Clinics," *Medical Care* vol. 11(1973), pp. 373–83; see also John B. Gangitano, "Health and the Low Income Family," *California Medicine* vol. 116 (1972), pp. 89–92.
4. These conclusions are based upon analyses of data collected by Wilbur H. Watson, on "Informal Social Networks in Support of Older Blacks in the Black Belt of the United States," (Washington, DC: National Center on Black Aged, 1980.) The data set consisted of 1727 cases on older blacks and whites who had lived most of their lives before 1965 in six states of the Southeastern United States, including North and South Carolina, Georgia, Alabama, Mississippi, and Louisiana. In addition to reporting upon their individual behaviors, the members of the sample were believed to be reliable informants about life styles in the local residential areas of the black belt where each had lived for a substantial proportion of his\her life.
5. Charles Watts (M.D.), professional history interview, Durham, North Carolina, 1986, pp. 9–10.
6. Robyn M. Dawes and Tom L. Smith, "Attitude and Opinion Measurement," pp. 509–566 in Gardner Lindzey and Elliot Aronson (eds.), *The Handbook of Social Psychology*, vol. 1, 3d ed. (New York: Random House, 1985).

7. Watts, p. 10.
8. Brooks.
9. Watts, p. 10; This observation was corroborated by Leroy W. Upperman (M.D.), professional history interview, Wilmington, North Carolina, 1986, p. 12.
10. Erving Goffman, *Interaction Ritual: Essays on Face-to-Face Interaction* (Chicago: Aldine, 1967), p. 5.
11. George Thomas (M.D.), professional history interview, New Orleans, Louisiana, 1986, pp. 10–11.
12. Brooks; see also Gangitano.
13. John C. Norman (ed.), *Medicine in the Ghetto* (New York: Appleton-Century Crofts, 1969).
14. Wilbur H. Watson, *Black Folk Medicine: The Therapeutic Significance of Faith and Trust* (New Brunswick, NJ: Transaction Publishers, 1984); see also Patrick A. Twumasi, *Medical Systems in Ghana: A Study in Medical Sociology* (Accra-Tema, Ghana: Ghana Publishing Corporation, 1975).
15. Watts, p. 28.
16. Upperman, p. 14.
17. For more detail on selected interrelations between biomedical and traditional medical practitioners, See Watson, *Black Folk Medicine*.

8

Stigma and Coping with Professional Degradation

Except that the character of an individual is known,
there can be no just appreciation of his worth, and as
with individuals, so is it with classes.
—Delaney (1864)[1]

The depth of the color line in the United States has shown nowhere more clearly than in the structure of perceptions of "self-alienated" blacks looking upon themselves and interacting with each other. It was not surprising during the period of separatism to find whites whose thoughts about race relations began with the assumption that they were superior to blacks and therefore it was proper for them to act with impunity and disregard toward blacks as human beings.[2] Far more tragic, was the evidence that some blacks had internalized separatist beliefs about blacks and in some instances turned against other blacks, symbolically expressing self-hate.[3] Some of the findings reported in the previous chapter on "doctor shopping," especially the pejorative attitudes of some black patients toward black physicians lend themselves to this interpretation.

This chapter focuses on a variety of occasions for social interaction that helped to set the stage for the degradation of black physicians but that were often met by resistance from them. First, there were occasions when whites showed their disrespect for blacks by dishonoring their statuses as physicians even when they were present. Secondly, there were occasions when a black patient, for whatever reasons, sought and/or accepted medical services from a black physician who was subsequently rejected by the patient when a white physician entered the scene. Instances of professional degradation growing out of each of these situations and others will be described. First, however, let us establish the nature of stigma.

A *stigma* is an attribute of individual or group character that signifies something "unusual and bad about the being of the signifier."[4] As many laws and social customs have shown in the history of the United States, being "black" signified something reprehensible about the bearer of that attribute even if the individual happened to be a physician. The bearer of this mark of identity was subject to the risk of social and psychological degradation.[5] Since the coming of the first African American in medicine in the United States, 1837, most black physicians have had first hand experiences with this kind of interaction. As in other walks of life in the United States, the color line has shown its ugly head in the social organization of medicine. First, we will consider instances in which racial identity was associated with value judgments about the competence of the physician.

Questioning the Competence of Black Physicians

In addition to the depth of *The Mark of Oppression* as described by Kardiner and Ovessy in their book by that title,[6] the following case illustrations represent an underlying belief—widely held among whites and some blacks under separatism and to some extent, in the present—that black physicians were not as well trained as whites. A black pediatrician commented on this problem.

> Well, the thing about it is they thought that we weren't trained as well as the whites. In spite of that belief, I imagine I was the only pediatrician at one time here who had a post-doctoral degree, you know, in pediatrics. But, that didn't make any difference. You would be surprised how ignorant some of the [white] professors were at the college, complaining about the training that black physicians had.[7]

The anguish that many black physician's felt was understandable, having academic achievements and specialized training—in some cases—that demonstrated their competence to be equal to or better than their white counterparts. Moreover, there were instances of professional degradation of black physicians by whites, often carried out in the company of other blacks and whites. For example, it was not uncommon for black physicians to be compelled to aid and abet less competent white physicians in the performance of medical practices following which the major credit went to the white colleague. The following account is illustrative:

I had a [black] patient, a child who had been going to a white physician and had been to the hospital, and they hadn't been able to make a diagnosis on this child. So, they brought the child to me, and I made that diagnosis of meningitis. And as soon as I made that diagnosis, they took the child back to the white doctor because they felt I wouldn't be able to treat meningitis. But since we knew what it was, the white doctor would be able to treat it.

Q: They assumed that you wouldn't be able to treat it? Yes, but I was able to diagnosis it when the others failed. Still, they took the patient back to treat it themselves after we knew what it was. So that shows you how they thought of black doctors.[8]

Another example of the subservience expected of black physicians in association with the color line is illustrated in the following case. The significance of this case is the decision made by the parents of the pediatric patient when two doctors were present, one black and one white, but only one treated the patient. This is an instance of a black physician who was summoned by a black family to make a home visit to treat a child who was seriously ill. The usual family physician was a white doctor who was not available when the family called. As a consequence, the family turned to a black pediatrician who was available and agreed to visit the home to treat the child. The following events transpired:

I had specialized in pediatrics, and a Mr. Coleman who was really frantic was describing the condition of the child and sounded as though the child had a serious disorder. So, I told the folks in my office, "I would like to go and see this child because it really seems like an emergency. And, of course they didn't go to the hospital for emergencies in those days. So, I went out there to see the child, and the child did have pneumonia. And we would have to treat the child at home. The child was in distress, and I treated him and made him fairly comfortable. The guy was about to pay me for the visit near the front door, and here comes Dr. Boone [the white family physician]. Since the patient's father didn't know me before this visit, he had started to pay me. Then he said, "can you wait for your money? I want to give this money to Dr. Boone." Dr. Boone called him a damn fool. And said, "this doctor has been here and treated your child, and evidently you're satisfied, since you were about to pay him. And you called me three days ago."[9]

What is observed here may symbolize a custom that can be expressed by the following rule that may have been operative in some localities: when a black and white doctor are co-present in the same time and place responding to a patient who needs treatment, the white physician's presence preempts the right of the black physician from receiving a fee or other kinds of credit for service even though he is (or was) the treatment physician-of-record. Further study is needed to determine whether or not this interpretation can be generalized to other comparable situations during the period of separatism.

Even when some families could not afford the fee, and could never-theless get a black physician to visit a home and accept delayed pay-ment, some family members would insist on borrowing the money to secure a white doctor. In some instances, "black medical care" was apparently reprehensible, even if it was free. Another example will help to drive the point home.

> Early one morning, about 1:00 A.M. or 2:00 A.M., the telephone rang. I answered. It was a woman who was quite upset about the condition of her child. And she wanted me to come out and see her child. So, a guy was in there loud talking [whom I overheard through the phone], and asked her who was she talking to. She said, "I'm calling [a black doctor] to see if he will come to see my child." And he said to her, "oh hang that telephone up, don't talk to that nigger doctor." She said, "look, this doctor will come to see my child if I don't have any money and let me pay him later." He said, "well, that ain't nothing; hang it up and go borrow some money and call you a white doctor." He said that loud enough for me to here it over the telephone. So, that's the type of thing we encountered.[10]

The challenges faced by black physicians to sustain a positive out-look as health professionals were frequent and often demoralizing. Yet, many survived the period, developed successful practices and fortu-nately lived to share their thoughts with students and professionals of the post-desegregation period. By studying the challenges and coping behaviors of our predecessors we can develop insights into the kinds of character ideals needed to take the next steps up from segregation and race-related degradation.

Blacks' Distrust of Blacks

Aside from the impact of race on interprofessional relations, some black physicians also had to contend with a lack of deference shown them by some black patients. A black physician provided an illustra-tion from his notes on attitudes toward black doctors by black women in Shreveport:

> When I first came here, a black female patient said to me, "'here are three things that a black doctor can do for me: fill out insurance blanks, perform an abortion, and treat a cold." Do you realize how, by keeping the black doctor out of training, he comes to a corner where he can only do three things? This is why I mentioned to you E. Franklin Frazier's, *Black Bourgeois*. Black Americans still have a seri-ous problem.[11]

Considering the use of physical examinations as diagnostic proce-dures, it was even more striking to find the intrusion of the color line in the perspectives of black patients on the diagnostic practices of black physicians. This case initially involved a woman who came to a doctor for the treatment of a cold.

> I told her I didn't treat colds. She said, "what about giving me a shot of penicillin?" I said, "if you are that good to know what you need, you go ahead and give it to yourself. However, if you want me to examine you, I will do a thorough examination, make a diagnosis and institute the treatment." The nurse put her there [on the examination table]. She said, "you, a black doctor looking under my dress!?" She screamed, and I had a waiting room full of patients. I wrote a letter to the people she worked for and who were taking care of her, and I made the white men responsible to have brought a black woman to think that way. Number one, she believes she's inferior, and she believes all blacks are inferior.[12]

Lest the reader be mislead into believing that the foregoing quotation reflects a repugnant attitude toward black physicians that may be peculiar to lower class blacks, I present the following counter-instance. While the following example may not represent the general case among middle-class blacks in attitudes toward black physicians, it does signify that class-standing and status climbing does not necessarily mean rising above or precluding the social psychological effects of the color line.

> The wife of one of the professors at North Carolina Central was a patient of mine. His wife was real sick. I admitted she was sick and everything. The President [of North Carolina Central] told this professor that he ought to get rid of me, and get his white doctor to treat his wife or else he was going to lose her. And he told him, "I don't give a damn if she dies. Dr. C. is going to treat her."[13]

It could be argued that this was another case of preference based on the belief of differential competence among physicians. But even if that were the case, it does not obviate the intrusion of the color line.

Coping with the Risk of Professional Degradation

Far from submissiveness in their responses to professional degradation, there was widespread evidence of group and individual protest by black physicians. Defiance of racially biased customs in many places, and displacement shown through discriminatory treatment of white patients was also reported. The development of private hospitals owned and operated by blacks for blacks was another important development of the late nineteenth and the first half of the twentieth centuries. These hospital facilities contributed, albeit modestly, to the development of comprehensive health care systems for African Americans in spite of separatism. Some of the outcomes of the latter developments are described in chapter 4 on "The Significance of Physician Access to Hospitals."

To be sure, all black physicians did not show identical strengths in their coping abilities. Some showed signs of despair. Often, "the going did get rough." Yet, few of the older physicians interviewed for this study remained downtrodden for long. None whom I interviewed reported abandoning the profession. Many shifted from attempts to stand alone against the multitude of white oppressors to joining racially aligned local, state, or regional societies or associations of blacks in the medical and allied health professions. The Old State Medical Society in North Carolina was an example of this kind of organization. Its membership was composed of physicians, dentists, chiropractors, and other health professionals brought together for the purpose of creating a critical mass more powerful than any single group of professionals standing alone. The National Medical Association, organized in 1895, was another group intended to help confront discriminatory treatment of black physicians.

It is clear that while requirements for competency in medical practice were standardized for physicians, both black and white, in the United States between 1896 and 1965, the actual practice of medicine varied considerably by locality, including urban areas and rural towns, north and south, east and west. Unlike my original hypothesis that the principle determinants of variations in medical practice would be local and regional differences in the enforcement of rules of racial separatism, the observed factors helping to account for variations in medical practices were much more complex. Crucial among the nonlegal factors were personality differences among physicians, variations among communities in traditions of race relations and etiquette, differential densities of black and white populations, and political influences of blacks and whites. While racism and interpersonal influence clearly made differences in the practice of medicine and even the opportunities that were available to black doctors, it was equally important to consider how each black doctor responded to those opportunities.

Interviews conducted through this study showed that some doctors responded proactively and tried deliberately to confront discriminatory practices of white physicians by inducing favorable changes in race and professional relations, for example, through medical associations in which they held membership and/or had some decision-making power. Developing black owned and operated hospitals under the aegis of black administrators was another way of countering the negative effects of segregation. In some cases, black doctors sought to gain membership on the staffs of predominantly white hospitals and, in addition to enhancing their own personal professional standing, used their positions to influence improvements for all blacks from inside the hospitals. Some sought to demonstrate that they were able physicians within their specialties and that they were equal to or more competent than their white colleagues.

In other instances, some black physicians avoided open competition with white colleagues. Yet others tried to adjust to the oppressive effects of separatism by attaching themselves to a senior black or white physician who had already established a successful practice. In the latter instances, the black physician would try to reap whatever benefits he could by working as a junior partner of an established practice. Finally, some black medical doctors withdrew from the medical profession itself, never having been able to establish a successful practice.

Conclusions

This chapter and the others in part 2 continued the exposure of the multifaceted social and psychological challenges faced by black physicians in the history of the United States. While most black physicians since 1900 earned their medical degrees and specialized training through an accredited and reputable medical school, many nevertheless had to cope with invasive public questions and/or doubts about their abilities to practice medicine competently. Often these doubts, as shown in this chapter, were not voiced. Instead, they were frequently symbolic in the social organization of medical practice and the statuses and responsibilities allocated (or denied) blacks, especially in racially mixed or integrated medical- service settings.

The specter of disbelief in the competence of black physicians was not necessarily an expression of pejorative judgment made by white physicians or patients. In some instances, black physicians and/or patients were the protagonists, themselves. As we have shown, distrust among blacks interfered in a variety of ways in referrals and in doctor-patient relationships. Unfortunately, there were no simple solutions to the problem of disbelief in the competence of black physicians.

Gaining credibility in the eyes of established colleagues; receipt of referrals of patients for specialized diagnoses and treatments; continuous professional growth through continuing and postdoctoral education and successful passage of board certified specialty examinations helped to build trust and fend off claims of incompetence. To help meet the challenges of race-related exclusions from medical associations, such as the American Medical Association (AMA), and other kinds of discriminatory treatment, many black physicians formed and/or joined other local, regional, or national organizations committed to the interests of black physicians and other health professionals who shared their outrage. The National Medical Association was formed in 1895 to foster their interests. For some, the NAACP became the advocate of choice along with membership in other groups.

We turn in part 3 to a discussion of social change, beginning with urbanization and the decline of the country doctor. Secondly, there are brief discussions of traditional medical beliefs and practices in the background of modern biomedicine, the points of view of black physicians on selected ethical issues pertinent to health care, and the contemporary status of black physicians.

Notes

1. Martin Robison Delaney, *The Condition, Elevation, Emigration and Destiny of the Colored People of the United States,* with a new preface by Benjamin Quarles (New York: Arno Press and *The New York Times*, 1969), p. 10.
2. Erving Goffman, *Stigma: Notes on the Management of Spoiled Identity* (Englewood Cliffs, NJ: Prentice-Hall, 1963).
3. Abram Kardiner and Lionel Ovessy, *The Mark of Oppression: Explorations in the Personality of the American Negro* (New York: Meridian Books, 1962).
4. Kardiner and Ovessy, *The Mark of Oppression.*
5. Gunnar Myrdal, *The American Dilemma*, vol.1 (New Brunswick, NJ: Transaction Publishers, 1996).
6. For a discussion of this phenomena, see Alvin Poussaint, *Why Blacks Kill Blacks.*
7. Alexander Clelland (M.D.), professional history interview, Durham, North Carolina, 1986, p. 10.
8. Clelleand, p. 11.
9. Clelland, p. 9.
10. Clelland, pp. 7–8.
11. Jean Brieire (M.D.), professional history interview, Shreveport, Louisiana, 1986, pp. 6–7.
12. Brieire, pp. 6–7.
13. Clelland, p. 11.

Part 3

Urbanization, Ethics, and Alternative Approaches to Health Care

Introduction to Part 3

In part 2, detailed attention was focused on the everyday lives of African American physicians. The insights developed were important to understanding the self-perceptions of physicians, patients, and their interrelationships in the health-care process. Also important to understanding the practice of medicine and doctor-patient relationships in a racially segmented society were the broader social, political and economic forces discussed in part 1.

While the period of legally sanctioned racial separatism in the health-care services ended with the 1965 amendments to the Hill-Burton Act, some problems for blacks have continued. Poverty and discrimination in access to services at the state and local level have been prominent among them. Along with the intensification of urbanization of the U.S. population, there has also been a general decline in, and growing concern about the quality of, and access to health care services for the poor and underserved.

Chapter 9 is devoted to the "Vanishing Country Doctor." The focus is on the declining presence of medical doctors in rural settings and small towns with special reference to the use of house calls as a technique of service delivery. One of the interesting findings is the relative absence of women among country doctors, suggesting a practice largely dominated by men. The general decline of country doctors closely parallels the demographic shift of whites and blacks in the United States from predominantly rural to predominantly urban populations, 1890 to 1920, and 1890 to 1950, respectively. One of the latent effects of these demographic changes has been the growing presence of a rural underserved population, so far as health care is concerned.

Another policy-related matter that was seldom mentioned by the physicians interviewed for this study was the practitioner of "traditional" or alternative, medicine and his/her consumers. In spite of the refusal by some physicians to recognize traditional or folk medicine as an alternative form of the healing arts, folk practitioners have persisted throughout the history of health practices in the United States. In fact, in some localities, folk practitioners owned and operated the only locally available hospitals, treated the same patients seen by some physicians and made referrals to the same. Alternative approaches to health care other than biomedicine are a fact of life in human groups, even though different practitioners may elect not to recognize each other. The social organization of this kind of coexistence among practitioners in health-care delivery will be the focus of our attention in chapter 10, as it was to some extent in chapter 7.

Ethical issues and differences among physicians abound today in such areas as the "right to life," "euthanasia," "living wills," the propriety of "organ transplantation" and other topics. Even before the post-separatist period or desegregation in medicine, following the 1965 revisions to the Hill-Burton Act, ethical issues were raised about the Tuskegee syphilis experiments. The relative absence of discussion of this topic in the pages of the *Journal of the National Medical Association* is ominous, but does not make the ethical issues less important. The fact is that black males were the guinea pigs in these experiments, albeit conducted by white physicians on the grounds of the Tuskegee Institute, ironically, a setting where black physicians were well represented, but seemed to have little to say publicly about these experiments until the 1978 exposé in *Ebony* magazine. These topics and others are addressed in the first half of chapter 11.

Another major set of problems, but not necessarily explained by the transition from the separatist to the post-separatist periods in medicine, was the growing frequency of malpractice claims, increases in medical practice insurance costs, and the repercussions of these events on the practices of medicine by black physicians. One of the interesting hypotheses developed in this study is the probable significance of physicians' practices in small towns and the functions of socially solidary relations between doctors and patients as buffers or safeguards against the risk of misunderstanding, distrust, and either demonstrable malpractice or claims of the same. This topic is developed in the second half of chapter 11.

Finally, health-care financing is a major problem of our times, with growing demands on public and private coffers. With the growth in the incidence of poverty and near poverty among blacks and other minorities, health-care financing at full cost has become especially difficult for many. No simple solutions appear on the horizon.. Medicaid for the poor and a variety of managed care organizations have emerged since the late 1960s. With these changes have come new professional and financial challenges for many physicians. These topics, along with the contemporary status of black physicians and issues pertaining to prospects for improvement in the quality of health care for blacks in the twenty-first century will be the focus of the closing discussions presented in chapters twelve and thirteen.

9

The Vanishing Country Doctor

*An understanding of the relation of medicine and
society requires a delineation of the course of the
changes in medical practice as American society
developed from a locally agricultural economy with
domestic handicraft production, to an urban indus-
trial economy, primarily characterized by factory
production with wage labor.... The adjustment of
medical practice to these new situations has, of
course, been greatly influenced by changes that have
occurred in the competence of the medical profession.
This competence has been derived from theoretical
understanding of the nature of health and disease,
improved techniques, higher licensing standards,
advances in medical education on all levels and the
significant influence of the hospital as the crucial
center for medical practice, research and education.*
—Stern (1959)[1]

Achieving medical education was a goal shared by a growing number
of blacks by the end of the nineteenth century. As shown in chapter 2,
these outcomes were facilitated in no small way by the rise of programs
of medical education following the Civil War. Nevertheless, many African Americans in medicine, especially those who aspired to be surgeons,
or who periodically needed the specialized diagnostic and supportive
services of hospitals, were highly restricted in opportunities and in the
quality of their practices because of racially segregated health care facilities. Largely as a consequence of these conditions, most black physicians were limited to house calls and small office practices until the rise
of black owned and operated hospitals in the early twentieth century.

These practitioners, sometimes referred to as "country doctors," char-
acteristically delivered services at the homes of patients and performed

minor surgical and other procedures in private offices. While white physicians were also well represented among country doctors, they were less constrained than blacks and moved readily into hospital based practices with urbanization and technological advances in medicine.

Among black physicians before 1965, major surgery and intensive care that required full hospital services was normally turned over to a white physician in areas where black owned and operated hospitals were not accessible. In addition to widespread racial segregation of hospitals, effectively precluding access to most black physicians with black patients who needed hospital care, there were at least three other important factors that helped to account for the prevalence of country doctors among black physicians from the Reconstruction period to World War II: (1) the presence of the majority of black Americans in rural residential settings considerably remote from the cities where major hospitals and medical centers had begun to develop; (2) the high incidence of poverty and lack of health care insurance among many prospective black patients that precluded access to medical service centers; and (3) a lack of means of transportation from rural residential areas to urban medical centers.

In addition to house calls as a major vehicle for health services delivery, the country doctor was highly likely to (a) reside in the same neighborhood or village of the people whom he served; the doctor and/ or his family of origin was highly likely to (b) have lived in the settlement of his practice for at least a generation; he was likely to (c) be married; to (d) know and be known by many of his patients on a first name basis; and (e) often allowed patients to pay for medical care by relinquishing to the physician a nonmonetary item of value to the patient, such as a peck of apples or corn; or livestock; or services such as house cleaning, cooking, or plowing and planting a field. In other cases, poor patients were permitted to pay whatever they could afford, and in some instances, no cost at all. Changes in the practices of medicine, especially the decline of the country doctor under conditions of modernization will constitute the primary focus of this chapter.

Modernization, the Development of Hospital- and Clinic-Based Medicine, and the Decline of Home Visits

Educationally, country doctors like all physicians were trained in the techniques and arts of biomedicine, but tend to live in non-metropolitan residential settings and included house calls as a major means of delivering services to patients. From the biomedical point of view, most country doctors also shared the perspective that illness is caused by a disease that is the result of heredity, infection, diet, a virus, or one or another set of environmental conditions and/or interactions among these factors producing malfunctioning in bodily processes.[2] Healthy behavior is conceived as a consequence of purposeful, adaptive responses to internal or external stimuli in everyday life, including disease conditions, whether those responses be physical, mental, emotional, or social.[3] In addition to the body's own processes that are naturalistically engaged to fight off disease, biomedical and traditional medical specialists through their knowledge and skills along with other health and allied health professionals may aid in the processes of sustaining healthy behavior and/or recovering well-being after a period of illness.

With the development of urban medical centers and the lure of better paying jobs, better laboratories, better equipped offices, and opportunities for lucrative private practices, there has been an increasing concentration of physicians in urban centers and a decreasing presence of country doctors in rural residential areas. The decline of home visits by medical doctors since 1900 in rural areas is illustrated in tables 9.1, 9.2, and 9.4.

In tables 9.1 and 9.2, as well as table 9.4, a distinction is drawn between the turn of the century and World War II, on the one hand; referred to as the period of urban development. During this period there were massive rural-to-urban migrations of populations in the United States. Table 9.3 is illustrative. By contrast, the period from 1940 to the present, is referred to as the modern period, when the population of the United States had become (or was in process of becoming) predominantly urban dwellers. It will be noted in table 9.3 that the majority of white Americans had become urban dwellers by 1920; whereas blacks did not show this distribution until 1950.

Interest in individual economic profit and technical support were not the only reasons for the relocation of medical doctors to urban centers and decreasing home visits in rural areas. The rapidly growing populations of urban areas, coupled with an increasing demand for medical services and slow growth in the production of new doctors also contributed to an increasing strain on the few available physicians to meet the needs of urban and rural settlements.

House Calls

Before the passage of the Social Security Act of 1935, the develop-

TABLE 9.1

The Relationship between Social Historical Period and Presence of Medical
Doctors in Predominantly Black and Rural Counties of Four Southern States:
Virginia, South Carolina, Alabama, and Georgia[1]

M.D. in Village	Virginia		South Carolina	
	Developmental (1901–1940)	Modern (1941–1980)	Developmental (1901–1940)	Modern (1941–80)
Yes	97%	15%	89%	30%
No	3%	85%	11%	70%
	29	27	27	27
	$(x^2=35, p < .05, 1df)$		$(x^2=20, p < .05, 1df)$	

M.D. in Village	Alabama		Georgia	
	Developmental (1901–1940)	Modern (1941–80)	Developmental (1901–1940)	Modern (1941–80)
Yes	94%	33%	65%	25%
No	6%	67%	35%	75%
	33[2]	9[3]	40[4]	40[4]
	$(x^2=3.58, p < .05, 1df)$		$(X^2=13, p < .05, 1df)$	

1 These tables represent samples of older black informants, 60–92 years of age, who reported
on aspects of community organization at two different points in time during their life histories
in selected rural residential areas of the state named in each table.
2 There were three "no answer" responses with reference to the period between 1901–1940.
3 There were 27 "no answer" responses for this period.
4 In each time period on which this study focused there were three informants who refused or
were unable to report any observations.

ment of visiting nurses services and other programs that provided for
home delivered health care and medical centers with ambulance services, many physicians and patients, black and white, had little choice
but to participate in the delivery and consumption of medical care
through house calls. A New Orleans physician made the following
observation:

> A lot of people just couldn't afford to go into the hospital who really needed to be
> there. So we [black physicians] did quite a few house calls.[4]

It was surprising to find that several black physicians reported having white patients who were treated through house calls in spite of
the color line. In some parts of the country, such as rural North Carolina and central Georgia before 1954, house calls by black physicians
to white patients were explained by the absence of any other physi-

TABLE 9.2
The Relationship between Social Historical Period and the Presence
of Medical Doctors in Southern and Northern Mississippi

M.D. in Village	Southern Mississippi[1]		Northern Mississippi[1]	
	Developmental (Before 1940)	Modern (1941–1980)	Developmental (Before 1940)	Modern (1941–1980)
Yes	86%	56%	85%	19%
No	14%	44%	15%	81%
	29[2]	25[3]	34	32[4]
	(x^2=5.95, p < .05, 1df)		(x^2=30, p < .05, 1df)	

1 These tables represent samples of 31 older black informants (southern Mississippi), and 34 older informants from Northern Mississippi, 60–92 years of age, who reported their observations about two different points in time of community organization associated with their life histories in subregions of the state of Mississippi.

2 Two informants were unable to report on this period.

3 Six informants were unable to report this period.

4 There were two informants who did not answer this question for the 1941–1980 period of this study.

cians but black physicians and referrals by other lay persons in the local area.

In some areas of North Carolina, black physicians were the only ones in the county. That was true in Georgia too; down in Monticello, Georgia. [There was an older black physician there with whom] I made rounds...in a little hospital. He had fourteen patients, only two of them were black. He was the best doctor in the county. In rural areas, black physicians have been treating white folks since the early part of the century.[5]

The shift in emphases from the home visiting country doctor to centralized practices, for example through hospitals, is partly indicated by the fact that even though a doctor in 1980 may have been present or may have lived in the same village as his patients, he or she was much less likely to make home visits than in the past when similar conditions prevailed (see tables 9.1 and 9.2).

Under conditions of "cracker culture," the decline of the country doctor during the period of racial separatism in the United States (1896–1965) meant an increasing dependency of many blacks, young and old, on the uses of the most accessible, immediately available, and affordable kinds of health care in times of illness. As pointed out in chapter 4 and throughout chapters 5–8, cracker culture required submissive behavior by blacks in the presence of whites. Moreover, blacks were compelled (or found it advisable in some instances), including physicians, to make every effort to establish a working relationship with a white sponsor to improve his/her chances of social mobility, however limited, within the constraints of the "color line." For many black patients living under these conditions, public health clinics, folk medicine practitioners (and the kinds of remedies peculiar to them) became the primary means of health care.[6]

Separatism and the Bearing of White Residential Out-Migration on the Country Doctor in the Rural South

As already suggested, the relocation by many doctors from rural to urban practices was associated with population shifts from rural to urban centers over the last 100 years. Table 9.3 shows change in the population of blacks and whites from 1890 to 1990 by subregions of the country. By 1890, six years before the *Plessy v. Ferguson* decision (1896), the majority of blacks and whites in the United States were still living in non-metropolitan regions of the country.

As noted above and shown in table 9.3, the majority of whites in the United States had shifted from rural to urban regions of the country by 1920. By contrast, the majority of black Americans did not show this shift in their distribution until 1950, 30 years later. It should be noted that, except for the period between 1940 and 1950, the great majority of the rural to urban migration of blacks and whites occurred before 1940, the year demarcating the developmental and modern periods shown in tables 9.1, 9.2, and 9.4.

It should be noted also that while table 9.3 shows a steady decline in the proportion of all whites in non-metropolitan relative to metropolitan areas of the United States from 1890 to 1990, there was also growth in the absolute numbers of whites within non-metropolitan areas over the same period of time. By contrast, with the exception of the period from 1890 to 1910 wherein blacks showed some growth in their absolute numbers in non-metropolitan areas, there was a steady decline in their proportions in non-metropolitan relative to metropolitan areas since 1890, and a decline in their proportions relative to all blacks within non-metropolitan areas since 1910.

Table 9.3 also shows that there were significantly more blacks than whites by proportion in non-metropolitan areas of the United States from 1890 to 1940 with only a minor difference between their proportions in 1950. During the period, 1940–1950, however, there was an

TABLE 9.3
Population Change in the United States, 1890–1990
by Metropolitan and Non-metropolitan Subregions and Race

Decennial Year	Total* Population	White Population				Black Population			
		Total White (TW)	Metro White	Non Metro White (NMW)	NMW as % of TW	Total Black (TB)	Metro Black	Non Metro Black (NMB)	NMB as % of TB
1890	62,424,345	55,101,258	19,317,550	35,783,708	.65	7,323,087	1,317,062	6,006,025	.82
1900	75,643,190	66,809,196	26,494,130	40,315,066	.60	8,833,994	1,810,250	7,023,744	.79
1910	91,559,720	81,731,957	39,831,913	41,900,044	.51	9,827,763	2,689,229	7,138,534	.73
1920	105,284,046	94,820,915	50,620,084	44,200,831	.47	10,463,131	3,559,473	6,903,658	.66
1930	122,177,883	110,286,740	63,560,033	46,726,707	.42	11,891,143	5,193,913	6,697,230	.56
1940	131,080,388	118,214,870	67,972,823	50,242,047	.42	12,865,518	6,253,588	6,611,930	.51
1950	149,984,314	134,942,028	86,756,435	48,185,593	.36	15,042,286	9,392,608	5,649,678	.37
1960	177,703,563	158,831,732	110,428,332	48,403,400	.30	18,871,831	13,807,640	5,064,191	.27
1970	200,329,264	177,748,975	128,773,240	48,975,735	.27	22,580,289	18,367,318	4,212,971	.19
1980	214,866,647	188,371,622	134,321,744	54,049,878	.29	26,495,019	22,594,010	3,901,009	.15
1990	248,886,000	208,754,000	159,554,000	49,200,000	.24	30,895,000	25,630,000	5,265,000	.17

*The figures in this column exclude all races, except blacks and whites.

Source: Data on the decennial periods from 1890 to 1970 were collected from the Historical Abstracts (Bicentennial Edition), U.S. Department of Commerce, Bureau of the Census, Colonial Times to 1970, Part I, n.d. Documentation for the 1980 population and subtotals are found in volume I, U.S Department of Commerce, Bureau of the Census, "Characteristics of the Population," Chapter A, January 1982, pps. 11–14. All of the 1990 data are from Claudette E. Bennett, Current Population Reports, Population characteristics, p.20–464. *The Black Population in the United States*, March 1991, p.133, Table 3. Washington, D.C.: U.S. Department of Commerce, Economics and Statistics Administration, Bureau of the Census, March, 1991.

acceleration of the growth of blacks in metropolitan areas (50 percent), far more rapid by proportion, than their white counterparts (28 percent). Partly as a consequence of this accelerated growth in urban centers, United States censuses of the aggregate populations have shown significantly fewer proportions of blacks than whites since 1960 in non-metropolitan settlements of the United States.

Since 1890, black Americans have changed from a preponderantly rural to an overwhelmingly urban population in the 1990s. This has been a key factor in the decline of the country doctor among blacks. While there has been a decline, as well, in the presence of white country doctors over the decades, the decline among whites in general has not been as dramatic as that shown among blacks.

Most of the doctors (about 97 percent) who were the objects of informant reports in this part of the study were white, as represented by tables 9.1, 9.2, and 9.4. The doctors represented by these tables migrated from rural to urban areas between 1901 and 1980. It should be recalled that all of the these doctors had practices in the rural areas of the states of Virginia, South Carolina, Georgia, Alabama, Mississippi, and Louisiana. And, given the nature of "cracker culture," it seemed reasonable that under conditions of massive white migration from a predominantly white community, a white doctor who was loyal to the beliefs, values, and rules of this culture would be highly likely to follow the migratory path of his/her former white patients, or at least find it uncomfortable if not socially intolerable to retain a practice in a village that was or had become predominantly black. To put it another way, some white doctors who provided home visits to blacks during the period of racial separatism may have done so because of a much larger white clientele that (1) also lived in the village and supported the doctor's practice; (2) approved or interceded from time to time to see to it that black domestic servants, field hands, and others received the health care that they needed to sustain life[7]; or (3) simply rewarded blacks from time to time with health care in exchange for being "good niggers."[8]

Some white doctors, however, may have developed a black clientele sufficient to support a practice and elected to remain in a racially changing neighborhood in spite of the prevailing beliefs and values that helped to define cracker culture.[9] This kind of symbolic resistance to cracker culture may have occurred under the following conditions: (1) the doctor found it less costly, economically, to retain his practice in the established locale, rather than move and start anew; or (2) the rules of cracker culture had become reprehensible and ignored by the white physician in favor of the higher calling of the profession of medicine.

An indirect test of the proposed significance of cultural bonds between separatist white residents and local white physicians, on the one hand, and out migration of whites from rural villages as factors helping to account for vanishing white country doctors was made possible through 234 sets of life history interview protocols available to this study. These data were collected from persons who had lived for one or more decades before 1940 in randomly selected rural residential areas of six of the southern states included in this study.[10]

The test was based on the assumption that the beliefs about the values of white solidarity implied in the etiquette of "cracker culture"[11] induced interpersonal attraction between white doctors and potentially white patients. By contrast, it seemed reasonable to expect that as the density of the white population declined in a given settlement, the remaining white doctor(s) who had internalized the etiquette of "cracker culture" would develop an increasing uneasiness with and/or repulsion toward their black patients, leading to significantly less interaction between them. Unless there was subsequent change in the rules for interaction between white doctors and black patients, it was expected that the white doctor(s) would relocate in the direction of his/her white clientele, thereby reinforcing the color line and their own economic gain.

Our investigation focuses on the extent to which white residents reported a loss of access to medical care that was similar in proportion to that reported by black residents of the same locality. As shown in table 9.4, the results indicated no change among whites when comparisons were made between their reported access to doctors in rural settings during their developmental years versus the modern period or later years of their lives. In contrast to whites, older blacks represented in table 9.4 reported a 51 percent decline in the presence of medical doctors who had previously made home visits to blacks in their communities.

The size of the samples in table 9.4 were too small to justify statistical tests of significances of the differences between proportions of doctors observed in the developmental and the modern periods. Nevertheless, the findings were suggestive, showing a marked decline among blacks, from 95 to 44 percent, who reported having a doctor who made home visits in his/her community.

The rules of racial separatism during the period between 1896 and 1965, requiring that blacks and whites avoid commingling, especially

TABLE 9.4

The Relationship between Social Historical Period and the
Presence of Medical Doctors in Rural Counties of Louisiana
as Perceived by Black (n=19) and White (n=9) Catholics

M.D. in Village	Black Catholics[1]		White Catholics[1]	
	Developmental (1901–1940)	Modern (1941–1980)	Developmental (1901–1940)	Modern (1942–1980)
Yes	95%	44%	89%	89%
No	5%	56%	11%	11%
19	18[2]	9	9	
	$(x^2 13. \; p < .05, \; 1df)$		$(X^2=0)$	

1 These tables represent two different samples of older black and white informants, 60–92 years of age, who reported on two different points in time of community organization associated with the histories in their subregions of the state of Louisiana, where they lived.

2 One member of the sample was either unwilling or unable to answer the question for this period.

but not exclusively in public places affected all domains of life as shown throughout this study.[12] To the extent that the beliefs and values about separatism were internalized by white physicians, it was reasonable to expect that a relocation of the white population from one community, where a doctor had established his practices, to another community where one or another white doctor was absent, would put pressure on the physician to relocate, but not necessarily follow the paths of migration of his previous white patients.

As we showed earlier, modernization of central business districts through the development of large, technologically well equipped hospitals; modern laboratory and research facilities, and higher wages for urban versus rural physicians were also factors helping to induce the relocation of physicians from rural to urban centers and the subsequent decline of the country doctor.

Other important factors included changes in public health laws since the turn of the century requiring that health care practices, such as obstetrics, midwifery and other specialties be implemented in germ free settings. These legalistic changes put increasing pressures on physicians to refrain from home visits, except for minor treatments. Additional pressure against the practice of medicine in unprotected or nonaseptic environments was brought by the growth of malpractice suits against physicians, and the increasing restrictions of insurance companies specifying the minimal essential environmental conditions, such as hospital settings within which medical care could be rendered without losing the protective shield of malpractice insurance.

Conclusions

Numerous social historical, economic, and cultural forces have contributed to the decline of the country doctor in the United States. While the central focus of this chapter was the rural southern United States, it is clear that the juxtaposition of the factors identified in the analysis of change in the distribution of physicians probably will have had similar consequences in other countries.

There are some exceptions to the conclusions that have been drawn about the decline of country doctors in general: (1) While the presence of white physicians in non-metropolitan areas has declined in general, especially in settlements that have become predominantly black, there have been some exceptions. Noteworthy has been the persistence of white physicians in non-metropolitan areas wherein a white clientele has remained in numbers sufficient to help support a medical practice; secondly, (2) black women physicians between 1896 and 1965 were primarily northern born and urban or metropolitan-based in their practices. These factors may help to account for the fact that most black women included in this study never established practices as country doctors. (It may be useful to review chapter 3 for a previous discussion of this topic).

Where there are rural pockets of poverty that have undergone the loss of physicians, there has often also been reason to believe that the quality of health care in those localities has declined over the years, but not necessarily because of poverty or the absence of physicians. For example, there are some recent findings that suggest a positive relationship between the presence of physicians in rural areas and instances of morbidity and mortality.[13] In other words, the greater the presence of physicians, the higher the reported morbidity and mortality. This finding may be an artifact of increases in the number of patients and diagnoses, not the mere presence of physicians. By contrast, the same research suggested an inverse association between the presence of nurses and reported cases of morbidity and mortality.[14] These unusual findings warrant further study.

In spite of the decline of the presence of the country doctor, some physicians still maintain practices in rural areas in many parts of the United States. To help stem the shortage of physicians in rural settings, some medical schools in cooperation with the United States Public Health Service have begun special recruitment programs to attract students from rural and urban areas with interest in medical education and developing practices in rural settings. This emphasis, for example, is one of the goals of the Morehouse School of Medicine, founded in 1978. The effectiveness of these programs remains to be seen so far as they work in recruiting, training, and retaining physicians in rural settings for more than a brief period after training.

It should also be noted that the decline of the country doctor will almost certainly compel an increasing presence in rural settings of alternative health care practitioners that were already widespread before the rise of modern biomedicine. The next chapter does not address this question directly, but does focus broadly on folk medicine and other alternative forms of health care.

There is little question about the importance of folk medical practitioners in the history of health care in small communities. Their acceptance, however, has varied crossculturally and within sociocultural systems by degree of modernization, development of biomedical understandings of disease, legal constraints through denial of licensing and other factors.[15]

While these practitioners are seldom thought of in association with the achievements and health care contributions of black physicians, folk medical practitioners have made important contributions to improving the overall quality of life of African Americans during and since the period of racial separatism. Note, for example in chapter 4 the contributions of midwives in the history of delivery of health care services through black owned and/or operated hospitals. Chapter 10 will focus on linkages between biomedical and folk medical practitioners reported by informants and documented in archival records and other sources. Also presented is a discussion of the significance of folk practitioners to an understanding of the social and cultural contexts of the practices of medicine by black physicians.

Notes

1. Bernhard J. Stern, *Historical Sociology: The Selected Papers of Bernhard J. Stern,* essay on "The Physician and Society") (New York: The Citadel Press, 1959), pp. 195–396.
2. Wilbur H. Watson (ed.), *Black Folk Medicine: The Therapeutic Significance of Faith and Trust* (New Brunswick, NJ: Transaction Publishers, 1984), p. 11; see also Andrew C. Twaddle and Richard M. Hessler, *A Sociology of Health* (St. Louis, MS: C.V. Mosby, 1977), pp. 47–56.

3. Wilbur H. Watson, *Aging and Social Behavior: An Introduction to Social Gerontology* (Belmont, CA: Wadsworth, 1982).
4. George Thomas (M.D.), professional history interview, New Orleans, Louisiana, 1986, pp. 8–9.
5. Charles Watts (M.D.), professional history interview, Durham, North Carolina, 1986, pp. 12–13.
6. Watson, *Black Folk Medicine*; see also Carroll J. Bourg, "A Social Profile of Black Aged in a Southern Metropolitan Area," pp. 97–106 in J.J. Jackson (ed.), *Research Conference on Minority Group Aged in the South* (Durham, North Carolina: Duke University Center for the Study of Aging, 1971).
7. Savitt, Todd L., *Medicine and Slavery: The Disease and Health Care of Blacks in Antebellum Virginia* (Urbana, IL: University of Illinois Press, 1978).
8. Walter Fisher, "Physicians and Slavery in the Antebellum Medical Journal," pp. 153–164 in August Meier and Elliot Rudwick (eds.), *The Making of Black America, Vol. 1: The Origins of Black Americans* (New York: Athenaeum, 1969).
9. M.C. Hill and B.C. McCall, "Cracker Culture: A Preliminary Definition," *Phylon* vol. 11, no. 3 (1950), pp. 223–231.
10. For more details about the method, write the author at The Morehouse Research Institute, Morehouse College, 830 Westview Drive S.W., Atlanta, GA 30314.
11. Hill and McCall, "Cracker Culture," p. 225.
12. Ibid.
13. Veronica Scott, "Major Physical Disorders among Older Rural Blacks," pp. 1–10 in Wilbur Watson (ed.) in *An Epidemiology of Life-Threatening Disorders among Older Blacks* (Atlanta, GA: Center on Health and Aging of Atlanta University, 1988).
14. Ibid.
15. Wilbur H. Watson and Robert J. Maxwell (eds.), *Human Aging and Dying: A Study n Sociocultural Gerontology* (New York: St. Martins Press, 1977).

10

Interfaces of Folk and Biomedical Practitioners

> *People everywhere must choose from the several*
> *possible courses of action available to them in*
> *attempting to treat illness. The question of choice*
> *becomes even more significant in non-Western*
> *settings where modern medical services, often only*
> *recently having become available, represent alterna-*
> *tives to longer established alternative medical*
> *practices and native curing specialists. This kind of*
> *medical pluralism is common in countries of the Third*
> *World, particularly in their rural communities. People*
> *in these settings have an especially varied set of*
> *options and must regularly choose from among two or*
> *more distinct systems of medical knowledge and*
> *practice in seeking treatment for an illness*
> —Young (1981)[1]

The practice of "traditional" or alternative medicine and health care giving, especially midwifery and herbal medicine have been widespread among African Americans throughout their history on the North American continent. The prevalence of these practices has in no small measure been accounted for by the cultural heritage of blacks, poverty, lack of knowledge of other means of intervention, and racially segregated communities.

Practitioners of alternative medicine, such as herbalists and midwives, and consumers of these kinds of services persist in the late twentieth century. It is also true that practitioners of biomedicine and their consumers have become widespread among African Americans and in many instances have largely supplanted activities of alternative medicine practitioners. Among the factors helping to account for growth in access to biomedical services and displacement of alternative medicine among blacks were (1) the acceleration of biomedical education for blacks after 1869; (2) the development and enforcement of new public health standards; (3) the oppression of some practitioners of alternative medicine, such as the decertification of midwives in selected counties of the United States; (4) urbanization, desegregation, and the rise of African American access to modern hospital systems and (5) the rise of health-insurance programs, such as social security disability benefits, making health care available to growing numbers of persons, including poor blacks. Nevertheless, proponents of alternative medicine are still widespread, especially, but not exclusively in rural areas.[2]

The Significance of Alternative Medicine

There is some evidence in the history of health care for blacks in the United States that midwives and other practitioners of alternative medicine, among whom women were major leaders, developed in large numbers to help meet the needs of health care that exceeded the supply of biomedical doctors during the twentieth century period of white separatism in the United States.[3] The lower costs of services of alternative healers also was an important factor contributing to an increase in the demand for their services. According to the materials contained in the archives of Hampton Institute, the Amistad Collection of Tulane University, the Moreland-Spingarn Collection of Howard University, Tuskegee Institute, and other sources, midwives and other practitioners of alternative medicine were also widespread, for similar reasons, from the period of chattel slavery through the Reconstruction period of the late nineteenth century in the United States. In fact, there is evidence that practitioners of alternative medicine continue to have considerable influence in health care in the late twentieth century.[4]

Under conditions of protracted poverty and racial segregation, self-help techniques, for example through home remedies and other folk medical practices were the only options available for many.[5] An eighty-four-year-old black woman in Macon county Alabama is more graphic:

Colored folks was brought up on these old home remedies. Like I tell you about this "fever grass"—humph (laughing) you know folks in the community—lot of them would make that fever grass and the same day, night and give it to them when one got up. Didn't have no doctors. These old home remedies. That's all I ever took. Right now, you know, I ain't never been to a doctor.[6]

Set against the background of the demographic and social changes described in chapter 9, this chapter is addressed to relations between folk and biomedical practitioners and their patients during the period of racial separatism. Largely because of segregation, black health care providers in many localities were compelled to pool their limited resources to achieve a common good: developing and sustaining the health of African American people and whites as well. For example, the only hospital in Georgetown, South Carolina between 1930 and 1960 was owned and operated by a black female midwife. Like most towns in the South during that period, black physicians with patients who needed hospitalization were restricted to black owned and operated hospitals, unless they had the endorsement of a white sponsor. Under these conditions, the black physician in need of a hospital was most likely to coalesce with the owner of the local black hospital as they did in Georgetown and Denmark, South Carolina, and in other towns.

Similarly, "drug store" doctors in New Orleans, who got their names through the operation of their practices through a back room of a drugstore in their neighborhood, often performed side-by-side with the operator of the "spiritual corner," usually an alternative medical practitioner in the area. Spiritual corner is a term sometimes used to refer to a small back room of a drugstore, or grocery store in a small town or inner city neighborhood where the consumer could (and still can), in some localities, find an assortment of folk remedies for nearly any illness or interpersonal condition.[7] Interpersonal conditions include problems of affect, such as disorders of "love-hate," fear of being overcome by an "enemy" or other aspects of interpersonal relations for which the individual seeks treatment. In a sense, the intra-office proximity of alternative practitioners, pharmacists, and physicians was the forerunner of modern groups of private health care practitioners, which are now quite common in many urban centers.

While referrals were not common between physicians and practitioners of alternative medicine, there was evidence of interaction among them. Midwives who delivered live births outside of hospitals sometimes called upon a local cooperating physician in the event of an emergency, such as hemorrhaging that she could not stop, a breach birth that she could not (or was afraid to attempt to) complete. In some states and counties, midwives, like modern physicians' assistants and nurse practitioners, were required by law to be formerly associated with a practicing physician.[8] One physician in North Carolina gave the following account:

Before World War II, midwives were widespread and much needed. After the war, they were less needed. There were requirements that they be related in some way to an obstetrician. It was county by county. Some [counties] did not have a doctor, so they would allow midwives to deliver babies with no doctor around.[9]

In some instances, the midwife would have to transfer the patient to full care of the physician to maximize the best health care outcome for the expectant mother. It should be noted, however, that there was no evidence of obstetricians ever making referrals to midwives.

Although it was uncommon in the accounts given by black physicians in this study, some did reveal cases of midwives who delivered babies in hospitals. The following is illustrative:

The [midwives] are not really generally allowed to deliver in hospitals. But they do in some [localities]. I think in most of the rural hospitals they do. They deliver under [a physician's] supervision as certified midwives.[10]

Physicians and Their Willingness to Credit the Work and Cooperate with Practitioners of Alternative Medicine

Many of the physicians interviewed for this study expressed disdain toward folk medicine. That was not surprising. It was expected, however, that there would be more respect and evidence of cooperation between these practitioners in coastal cities of the southeastern United States where there was evidence of survivals of Africanisms among black Americans.[11] We did find indicators of cooperation, although not often mutual among physicians and folk practitioners in Georgetown and Charleston, South Carolina; Savannah, Georgia; Mobile, Alabama; New Orleans, Louisiana; and the Delta region of Mississippi. The data, however, were inconclusive. Further study is needed.

Some of the medical doctors interviewed for this study clearly indicated their respect for folk medical practitioners especially midwives in child-birthing activities. There were some who also indicated their acceptance of referrals of patients from midwives, although that was done informally, not with the approval of the medical profession. Different attitudes toward folk practitioners may be related to the cultural backgrounds of the physicians and the means by which they were born and reared, that is whether or not they were themselves delivered and taught to believe in and value the work of midwives. On the other hand, the presence of a respected practitioner of alternative medicine in the same town wherein the physician had come to establish a medical practice might also induce a positive or tolerant perspective on the work of the folk practitioner. The following anecdote drawn from an interview with a physician in the state of Virginia is illustrative:

> We had many midwives. In fact, the health department had classes for midwives. In those days, [before desegregation], the majority of the babies were delivered by midwives. And they [the babies] got check-ups from us; we had to give them certificates saying that their blood pressure and their urine were within normal limits for the midwives to deliver them. We also had a Dr. Hall who was a practitioner of folk medicine out in Chuka County. Dr. Hall was a good friend of ours. Many a man or woman came to see us because Dr. Hall had sent them. Dr. Hall recognized his limitations. Even though he did his incantations in his type of medicine, he was smart enough to know that he couldn't cure gonorrhea, which was a very popular thing. He would tell them, along with what he did, it wouldn't work unless the patient went to see a doctor and got a dose of penicillin. So there was a symbiotic relationship there. I thought he [Dr. Hall] was a smart man. He's been dead for a long time.[12]

This passage establishes the close working relation between a physician and two folk medical practitioners, and features of the mutual respect that helped to form a bond among them.

With the declining presence of country doctors in the late twentieth century, it seems reasonable to expect a resurgence of alternative medical practitioners and other healers in rural areas. Growing numbers of physicians' assistants, nurse practitioners and certified nurse midwives will be included. The shortage of professional and certified health care providers will no doubt lead to an influx of other healers in spite of their non-certification in some localities.

Conclusions

While the practice of alternative medicine helped to frame the historical background and sociocultural context of the practice of modern biomedicine, we have shown that practitioners of alternative medicine did not in all settings have direct interaction with physicians. In most historical periods wherein they coexisted, alternative healers and biomedical practitioners may have been in similar localities, but had little communication among them, especially referrals, except when the folk practitioner, such as a midwife, experienced difficulty in selected procedures, such as resolving a breech birth. Secondly, these relations seemed primarily asymmetrical: referrals were nearly always made by the alternative to the biomedical practitioner, but never the reverse.

It is also clear that the organization of alternative medicine was a source of support for black patients who in some instances, especially in rural, poor, remote residential settings without a physician had no alternative means of primary health care. In addition, the practitioners of alternative medicine in remote rural and some urban settings were often close confidants of black residents, often better known and more trusted, with their advice frequently sought in times of illness before the patient would select other kinds of care, such as that of a physician. In this regard, the practitioner of alternative medicine sometimes served as an intermediary between the patient and the physician, giving advice that often determined whether or not the patient sought professional biomedical care.

As intermediaries who made referrals, even though not reciprocated by their biomedical counterparts, the alternative medicine practitioner both acknowledged his or her limitations and reinforced the specialization and the authority of the physician. In this sense, the practitioner of alternative medicine clearly functioned as a source of professional support for the physician, no less true of white than black, although the relationships among them during the period of racial separatism may have been more open with stronger bonds between blacks than between blacks and whites.

Further, as shown in chapter 4 and reiterated somewhat in this chapter, some local hospitals were owned and/or operated by practitioners of alternative medicine. In those instances where physicians needed hospital beds to treat a serious illness or to perform surgery, they had no choice but to cooperate with the hospital administrators in spite of their disbelief in alternative medicine. Perhaps because blacks often had to practice medicine under these conditions, the worldviews of many gradually developed into forms of holistic medical perspectives. In an holistic framework, the patient is not merely an organism with a disease to be treated, but a multidimensional being who is approached with the understanding that body, mind, and significant social others are interactive and must be taken into account in the treatment process.

Notes

1. James Clay Young, *Medical Choice in a Mexican Village* (New Brunswick, NJ: Rutgers University Press, 1981), p. 3.
2. Judy Barrett Litoff, *American Midwives: 1860 to the Present* (Westport, CT: Greenwood Press, 1978).
3. Wilbur H. Watson, *Black Folk Medicine: The Therapeutic Significance of Faith and Trust* (New Brunswick, NJ: Transaction Publishers, 1984).
4. Ibid.; see also Litoff, *American Midwives.*
5. William T. Forrester (M.D.), professional history interview, conducted by Margaret Barnes, research associate, Richmond, Virginia, 19 May 1986, pp. 6–7.

6. Watson, *Black Folk Medicine,* p. 54.
7. Watson, ibid., p. 57.
8. Litoff, *American Midwives,* pp. 9–13. The practice of midwifery by women, primarily, and men secondarily was the predecessor to modern obstetrics. During the nineteenth century the presence of men as midwives grew rapidly. With the introduction of forceps as a tool to facilitate birthing, used nearly exclusively by male midwives, increasing conflict developed between males and females. As the profession of biomedicine grew and male midwives become more prevalent, women midwives experienced an increasing displacement by men identified with the new twentieth-century specialty called obstetrics. Men so identified became the key performers of child-birthing activities under the name of this new specialty of modern biomedicine.
9. Charles Watts (M.D.), professional history interview, Durham, North Carolina, 1986, p. 9.
10. Ibid., p. 9.
11. Mellville Herskovitz, Jr., *The Myth of the Negro Past* (Boston: Beacon Press, 1990), pp. 245–246. The question of the survival of "Africanisms" among New World blacks remains controversial. Herskovitz suggested that blacks in New World settlements developed by French and Catholics seemed to foster the survivals more and/or longer than others. My analysis suggests that these were for the most part on the fringes of the plantation South, the coastal areas and a selected few other localities not favorable to the political economies of plantations.
12. Margaret Reid (M.D.), professional history interview, conducted by Margaret Barnes, Norfolk, Virginia, 7 April 1986, p. 9; see also Joseph J. Quarles (M.D.), professional history interview, conducted by Margaret Barnes, Norfolk, Virginia, 13 May 1986, pp. 6–7.

11

Ethical Issues in the Practice of Medicine

> *The medical profession, up until the post-World War
> II period, was considered a "calling" almost like a
> priesthood; not only by the general public, but by
> physicians themselves. We are reminded almost daily
> of changes in the public attitude since then as the
> struggle to contain the malpractice awards problem is
> continuously in the news. Physicians appear unable
> to continue to care for patients in an effective and
> efficient fashion with this specter hanging over them.*
> —Message (1986, p. 1)[1]

There is no shortage of issues pertinent to the decisions that physicians must make on matters of life and death in the everyday routines of their practices. Frequently included are whether or not to remove from an individual a life-support system, such as a dialysis unit or a pacemaker, when that individual is "cerebrally dead" and would have little chance of continued expression of vital signs in the absence of these modern technological devices. Or, whether or not a physician has a right to deny a woman an abortion because that practice is against the physician's religion. In recent years the issue of "doctor-assisted suicide" has become a hot topic. There are, of course, many additional issues, some of which will be developed in the pages that follow.

It should be noted at the outset that it is not my intention to take sides on the issues raised. Instead my aims are to describe (1) the differing points of view on selected issues through documentary information provided by physicians interviewed for this study, and (2) the political and economic conditions that helped to shape the issues in recent years. Through an interpretation of the associations among these factors, the analysis will contribute insights into the humanistic characteristics and challenges of black physicians who (a) engaged in

143

the practice of medicine under conditions that were often less than humane for them and their patients, and (b) who were sometimes treated and/or self-perceived as outsiders relative to decision making on such matters as the Tuskegee syphilis experiments, putatively carried out in the interest of advancing the science and practice of medicine. Finally, a discussion is presented focusing on selected ethical, economic, and social significances of allegations of malpractice and malpractice suits.

The Tuskegee Syphilis Experiments

One of the clearest signs of the denial of importance of the points of view of black physicians was their exclusion by whites from deliberations on matters affecting black patients and health professionals, even in a town like Tuskegee, Alabama, the home of the fabled Institute by the same name. Tuskegee also claimed the first Veterans Administration Medical Center in the United States established initially for black veterans (1923), and the John A. Andrew Hospital and School of Nursing that became well known for its annual clinics for black physicians. As ironic as it may seem, from the vantage point of critical investigative journalism and social and health science inquiry of the 1980s and 1990s, many black physicians revealed to me that they were simply not aware of the Tuskegee syphilis experiments until many years after that study had begun. In fact, several physicians revealed to me that they first became aware of the experiments through an article in *Ebony Magazine* (1972),[2] nearly forty years after the inception of the experiments. These insignia of information control and/or ignorance help to signify the extent of the exclusion of black physicians and the editors of one of their major sources of news, *The Journal of the National Medical Association*.

Among physicians who were familiar with the experiments at the time of their implementation, or who became aware later through secondhand information, there were many differing points of view. There were those who unequivocally thought that the Tuskegee syphilis experiments were reprehensible and should never have been undertaken.[3] One physician, however revealed a broad outlook on medical experimentation, seeing the necessity of this kind of experimentation for the advancement of scientific knowledge and clinical interventions even though, in some instances, he found grounds for criticism because of abuses of human subjects.

I'm ambivalent. If I'm going to be objectively fair, I think that at the time things are done, people are concerned with the search for truth. Now, there have been some abuses and all. Go back to the dogs. If they hadn't experimented with animals, there are a lot of things that we would not know. At the time of the syphilis experiments, apparently, the greatest amount of syphilis was among blacks, and this was a good place to do the experiments. I remember years ago that many insurance companies wouldn't insure blacks; but some companies did because blacks were a high risk for tuberculosis. Insurance companies found out that tuberculosis was a problem of poverty and malnutrition. This was brought to light by research. I think if they were to make scientific studies now, they would do it in keeping with the information that we have today. I'm sure that they gained a lot of information. I don't believe that it [the Tuskegee experiments] were designed to be insulting to blacks. If people are going to take that attitude, well perhaps they're a little short sighted. That's my honest view. At Howard, when we had cadavers for the session, they were all black. The only way to get them was when derelicts died. Now, to dissect a black cadaver under those circumstances, I think was unavoidable. That's all I'm saying.[4]

There was considerable range of thought among early twentieth century black physicians on proper modes of belief and behavior in the practice of medicine. Perhaps, the view closest to the classical Hippocratic frame began with the following proposition:

As long as there is breath, it is unethical for any doctor to consider "mercy killing." The same thing applies to abortion. We're trying to preserve life. Abortion is an ethical antithesis.[5]

Reasoning along the same lines, some doctors thought the Tuskegee syphilis experiments improper because: (1) they threatened human life by permitting patient exposure to a disease without treatment, especially the withholding of a demonstrated intervention long after the necessary medical advances (penicillin in 1940) had occurred; and (2) engaged the use of human beings, albeit African American males, as guinea pigs.[6] It was interesting that in a number of interviews, the doctors' primary criticism did not flow from the premise that: the patients of the Tuskegee experiments were black, the doctors were white, and therefore the experiments were wrong. Instead, the argument was, the experiments were wrong because they were life-threatening, not life-saving, and antithetical to the ideals of science and medical practice, a conclusion that would have held truth value among physicians and laymen today, in all likelihood, regardless of the race or culture of the patients.

On Life-Support Systems

In a recent interview with a retired black physician in Wilmington, North Carolina, references were made to the "unburied dead."[7] By this term, he referred to patients who require life-support systems to keep vital organs functioning, such as the heart, lungs, or kidneys in the absence of which the individual would die. Further, this physician thought that it was improper for physicians or for anyone to interfere with the normal functioning of the body, even if that was motivated by the decline of vital signs. It is the duty of the doctor to work in harmony with and to support *natural* life giving systems, but not to intervene except to prevent death or exacerbations of illness conditions that may be a result of injury or disease.

> If you see all of what it takes to sustain vegetables in institutions, that begs the question [of the case for life support systems]. To me, my personal philosophy is that as long as a man is awake, sober, not insane or under anesthesia, satisfying his mind is all that is there. And once that's gone, carrying it on for years, and years, and years is just an expression of somebody's concern about you. I think they waste too much money on life-support systems.[8]

This physician noted that not only was he a pragmatist, but as a physician he had to be. He had to be primarily concerned with what works in the medical profession, not necessarily with what he idealized as a black physician practicing in the South.

Another physician in Durham, North Carolina expressed similar sentiments. His overriding point of view was that physicians should not engage in treatment that "prolongs the dying and suffering" of the patient.[9] He described the following case to illustrate his point of view.

> I had a patient whose parents I asked to please get another physician if they did not agree with my philosophy. This was a hydrocephalic. This is at birth. The brain was abnormally small. It looked like a bud where a brain should have been. The child had spina bifida. I told the parents that I was not going to put forth any heroic efforts to prolong this child's life, and that I would like for them to get another physician if they wanted such measures taken. I was able to get out of it without them making a decision because I told them that I would keep the child comfortable. The funny thing was until it was transferred, I kept it [the child] drunk. I'm an old physician, and we used to use alcohol in babies. I was able to get consultation. The consultant was in neurology. And he was probably anxious to do some surgery, which was not for the benefit of this particular child. This child might, however, receive some benefit from it. I mean, it [the benefits] couldn't be permanent because it didn't have a brain in the first place to do anything except those instinctive things, which were initiated in the spinal cord. The child was under this doctor's care when it died.[10]

The "Right to Life"

Closely related to the ethical issues associated with life-support systems is the "right to life" controversy. Here the major focus is on the "rights" of the unborn over against the rights of a woman to have her pregnancy interrupted, for example by abortion. The following quotation shows the position of a physician who argues that right to life advocates should temper their judgments with considerations of the kind and quality of life into which the child will be born.

> I'm not a "right to life" advocate. I was with the Health Department every since I've been here. And I've been on the Board of Directors and had charge of the children's clinic for years. In fact, I just retired from that not long ago. And I saw more children with the County Health Department than all other physicians combined. Seeing how those kids were inadequately fed and stuff like that, I said it would have been much better for them to have never been born...to come into that. And I don't see how these "right to life" people would want these folks to come here and starve to death. I mean, a slow death. They don't give a rap about them after they are born.[11]

This physician went on to state that economic hardships, poor health, and childhood pregnancies are some of the conditions under which rights to abortion should be given favorable consideration.

> That [abortions] was one of the things I was fighting for at the Health Department. We actually funded abortions. I had one girl eleven years old when she had her first baby. Before she reached her twelfth birthday, she had a second child.[12]

Clearly, the right to life versus the right to abort raises complex issues on each side of the debate. Another domain of ethical issues that affect most physicians in their personal practices pertains to questions of "malpractice," or allegations of improper conduct of the physician in the process of using the tools of his trade.

The Nemeses of Medical Malpractice Suits

The risk and fear of suits against physicians for malpractice are topics of considerable concern among all medical doctors, regardless of race. This concern, however, does not seem to grow out of a fear of having wrong doings uncovered, but the increasing costs of malpractice insurance and the subsequent risk of being driven out of professional practice because of exorbitant, unaffordable costs.

Social and Economic Determinants of Malpractice Suits

Several doctors in this study independently agreed that alienation of patients from doctors and the exploitation of distrust by modern lawyers have contributed significantly in recent years to growth in malpractice suits.

> If America returned to the concept of family physician, instead of practicing strictly nuclear medicine, where the patients come to the doctor, [after] all sophisticated tests have been done, such as laboratory tests and x-rays.... If they [doctors] come back to establish a rapport—warm rapport, all that problem [alienation] will be solved. The patient is a human being who wants a warm human touch, consideration, love and kindness. That patient wants the doctor's time and knowledge.[13]

One of the best tests of this proposition is the difference between experiences of physicians in rural and urban settings. Independent interviews of rural, small town, and urban physicians in this study tended to support this hunch. According to a physician in Shreveport, Louisiana, rural physicians "don't have those [malpractice] kinds of problems."[14]

Adjusting to the Risk of a Malpractice Suit

Acquiring protection through the purchase of malpractice insurance was a clear way of diminishing the potential economic damage of a successful malpractice suit. This means of protection, however, was not easily accessible to every physician who needed it. The cost was often prohibitive. As a consequence, some physicians elected to give up private practice for a lower fixed income and a malpractice insurance policy provided by a corporate employer, such as a hospital.

> A lot of them are retiring early; a lot of them are going into other fields and even though they don't do that, everybody's looking for a job now, they want to work for somebody. Working for an HMO or PPO and working for a university or on a hospital staff as an instructor or as a house physician, then they [the host institution] suffers the cost, you know; the malpractice insurance and everything.[15]

According to a recent article in the *New England Journal of Medicine*, the growing preferences by individual physicians to elect institutional positions over private practices, as suggested in the foregoing quotation, is consistent with a movement in the United States to assign all costs of malpractice insurance to the hospital corporation under whose auspices the physician practices.[16] This article also draws attention to the fact that 80 percent of all malpractice claims arise out of events occurring within hospital walls.[17] In spite of the latter observation, however, insurance companies tend to spread the costs over all health professionals covered by the companies, even though a particular individual may be primarily in private practice with little or no history of malpractice claims against him or her.

Malpractice claims have become so serious a problem for physicians, and mal-practice—insurance premiums are rising so high in proportion to the income of physicians, that leaving the situation as it is has become untenable.... Economics of scale are achieved by concentrating insurance coverage in the corporate structure rather than individualizing costs and claims reserves around each practicing physician....[18]

One older physician expressed his concern that the continuing growth in malpractice suits and growth in insurance costs for physicians will contribute to a reduction of new black physicians entering the profession, especially the high-risk specialties, such as obstetrics and gynecology.

I have a dim view of blacks ever assuming their correct percentage of expression in the medical area. The reason for that is what it takes to prepare yourself for medical school..., then when they get there [into practice], there are problems of getting a residency for the specialty, referrals from white doctors, and...malpractice insurance that they can't afford.[19]

Although this is a brief discussion of selected ethical issues, the challenges that await new and older black physicians are manifold. With the historical processes of urbanization, population movements, bureaucratization of professional relations and risks of doctors alienation from patients, the return to primary group relations of small towns seems unlikely. That the modern day physician is likely to be a stranger, not the familiar caregiver previously represented by the "country doctor," is probably a forgone conclusion.

Conclusions

This chapter raises questions about several ethical issues that have been of great moment to black physicians in the United States. In spite of the analytic focus of this study on the period of racial separatism, it is clear that the Supreme Court decision of 1954 and the amendments to the Hill-Burton Act in 1965 did not bring an end to debate on these issues. It is also acknowledged that this chapter at best scratches the surface of the issues that may matter to physicians, black, white, or other.

The problem of abiding by the Hippocratic oath has been an issue of recurrent discussion since the idea of the oath was first formulated. Similarly, the "right to life" debate is centuries old, although the lines between the antagonists have been hardened in recent decades with advances in the biological sciences, genetic engineering, especially the growth in our understanding of prenatal vital signs and amniocentesis (which now permits detecting a heart beat and determining sex of the fetus by the third or fourth month of pregnancy) and new thought on the philosophy of "human" beings.

More contemporary are the issues centering around "life-support systems" and medical experimentation, such as the questionable use of human subjects in the Tuskegee syphilis experiments. With the development of artificial lungs and hearts, pacemakers, and dialysis machines to support malfunctioning hearts, kidneys, and other organs many humanistic issues have arisen about the uses of these kinds of interventions. Included among the issues have been, how long should artificial life supports persist considering costs to individuals, families, and society. Secondly, after other vital organs have failed, such as the brain, and the surviving patient-person is declared "brain dead" should interventions then be withdrawn?

With the growing importance of finding answers to pressing questions about perplexing chronic and costly illnesses among human beings, and the questionable values of the results of experimentation using animals, more and more attention has turned to human experimentation, such as fetal tissue research. These developments have provoked increasingly sensitive and difficult questions about the rights of human subjects in scientific research. It is in this domain that the Tuskegee syphilis experiment was an object of inquiry in this chapter.

None of these topics lend themselves to easy or simple answers. Nor was it my intention to seek definitive conclusions through this chapter. Studies of the history of ethics and inquiry in this area have seemed more appropriate as a means of sensitizing each new generation to the humanistic issues of the past and present, and those worthy of contemplation as the future unfolds in the health sciences, especially the practice of medicine.

One of the changing features of the medical profession has been the social organization of service delivery. Change in this area has occurred in part, because of increasing densities of populations in urban areas, costs of new technology, and the delivery of services to patients. Modernization has included the centralization of services through the formation of complex medical service centers and the growth of managed care organizations.

Since the mid-twentieth century, the pace of each of these movements—urbanization, the centralization of service delivery through medical centers, and the development of managed care organizations—has accelerated. "Solo" country doctors have given way to urban physicians in group practices or to those who have become affiliated staff members of one or more of the new medical service centers.

The contemporary status of black physicians is the focus of chapter 12. Affirmative action and its critics, access to medical education and growth in the number of black physicians, desegregation, diversity in doctor-patient relationships, services to the poor and underserved, and the challenges of managed care are among the topics of discussion.

Notes

1. Message from the Director, "The Malpractice Crisis: Its Impact on the Elderly," *Update-Newsletter, Center for Aging*, University of Alabama at Birmingham vol. 5, no. 3 (Spring 1986), pp. 1–6.
2. George Thomas (M.D.), professional history interview, New Orleans, Louisiana, 1986, p. 26; see also Cornelius Johnathan Beck (M.D.), black physician, professional history interview, Georgetown, South Carolina, 13 October 1986, pp. 32–33. For the substance of the article, which helped to inform the public about these experiments, see Jack Slater, "Condemned to Die for Science," *Ebony,* vol. 28, no. 1 (Nov. 1972), pp. 177–193. See also *Bad Blood*, by James H. Jones (New York: The Free Press, 1993).
3. Fredrick Fundernberg (M.D.), professional history interview, Atlanta, Georgia, February 1985, p. 19; see also George Thomas (M.D.), professional history interview, New Orleans, Louisiana, 1986, p. 26.
4. Leroy W. Upperman (M.D.), professional history interview, Wilmington, North Carolina, May 1986, pp. 21–22.
5. Jean Breire (M.D.), professional history interview, Shreveport, Louisiana, 1986, p. 20.
6. Breire, p. 19.
7. Upperman 1986.
8. Upperman, p. 22.
9. William Clelland (M.D.), professional history interview, Durham, North Carolina, 6 June 1986, p. 20; see also Beck, p. 34.
10. Clelland, pp. 19–20.
11. Clelland, p. 25.
12. Ibid., pp. 25–26.
13. Breire, pp. 16–17.
14. Breire, p. 17.
15. Thomas, p. 17.
16. William J. Curran, "A Further Solution to the Malpractice Problem: Corporate Liability and Risk Management in Hospitals," *The New England Journal of Medicine* vol. 310, no. 11 (15 Mar. 1984), pp. 704–705.
17. Ibid.
18. Ibid., p. 705.
19. Upperman, pp. 25–27.

12

Contemporary Status of Black Physicians

*Our African-American "M.D." is now a practicing
physician who has been educated during the age of
integration. He or she may not believe in the necessity
of civil rights and may believe that he or she has
already been afforded the same advantages as the
majority physician. To be a committed physician
requires a willingness to educate oneself about the
many dimensions of managed care and the ability to
impart this knowledge to other minority physicians.
You must understand the multifacets of managed care
and that the "positioning" of minority physicians in
that arena is vital to most physician's livelihoods.
Unfortunately, too many of our physicians do not
clearly understand the significance of managed care.*

*Moreover, all committed candidates must be able to
work at the local, state, or federal level to negotiate
some type of universal health-care legislation
and thereafter to address in a timely manner
all future legislative needs for our patients.
We must indeed become political players*
—Veal (1995, pp. 529–530)

The general population of blacks in the United States grew steadily
from 1790 to 1990. Growth in the proportion of black physicians, however, did not keep pace. While blacks as a percentage of the total population of the United States had reached 12 percent by 1990, as a
percentage of all physicians in the civilian labor force, they represented
only 4 percent (see table 12.1).

By 1990, conservative estimates placed the number of physicians in
the civilian labor force at 515,565. This number is based upon data
reported by the U.S. Bureau of Labor Statistics documented in table

TABLE 12.1
Physicians by Race in the Civilian Labor Force, 1990

	White	Black
Male (414,886)	97%	3%
Female (100,679)	93%	7%
Totals (515,565)	494,027	21,538

Source: U.S. Bureau of Labor Statistics and Bureau of the Census, 1990. The findings in this table closely correspond to the estimates for black physicians by gender in table 11 reported in the Federal booklet on *Estimates and Projections of Black and Hispanic Physicians, Dentists and Pharmacists to 2010*. USDHHS, PHS, HRSA, May, 1996.

It should be noted that this table understates the number of civilians sixteen years of age and older who reported working as physicians during the 1990 Census of the U.S.. The number employed in this category was estimated at 586,715. For more detail see the *Statistical Record of Health and Medicine* edited by Charity Ann Dorgan, NY: Gale Research, 1995. There was no breakdown by race or gender.

Statistical Reporting on physicians leaves much to be desired. In another source on practicing physicians by country in 1990, it is reported that there were 601,100 physicians in the U.S. See USDHHS, HCFA, *Health Care Financing Review*, vol. 13, no. 4 (Summer 1992), p. 45. Unfortunately, this source made no differentiation by race and gender.

12.1. As shown in the footnotes to table 12.1, it is acknowledged that other sources for the same year estimated the number of physicians in the United States to be as high as 601,100.

Nevertheless, the U.S. Bureau of Labor Statistics was selected as the primary source for table 12.1 because, unlike the other sources acknowledged in the footnotes of the table, it differentiated the number of physicians in 1990 by race and gender, each of which were central objects of analysis in this study.

Black Physicians in Professional Associations

One of the most important questions about the contemporary status of black physicians is the extent to which they have been integrated into professional organizations of physicians and health care delivery organizations since desegregation. That sizable numbers would be members of the National Medical Association , founded in 1895 to promote the interests of black physicians was fully expected. In 1969, the NMA reported a membership of 5048 physicians.[1] By 1997, the NMA membership office reported an estimated 22,000 physicians.[2]

In my attempt to compare NMA growth to that among black physicians in the American Medical Association, a reasonable indicator of desegregation, I was less successful. Of the broadly based public records, such as publications on AMA membership and U.S. Census reports, few insights were provided. Some historical studies showed that black physicians could not easily gain membership in local chapters of the AMA, even when that was their preference.

During the first half of the twentieth century, according to Starr's analysis,[3] the AMA became increasingly concerned about its control of hospital appointments in the United States and the mobility of physicians. To help institutionalize its control of these outcomes, the AMA promoted a requirement that all hospitals accredited for internship training appoint no one to their staff positions except members of the local medical society affiliated with the AMA. Since black doctors were excluded from the local medical societies in many states, they were also excluded from many hospital positions on those grounds.[4] As a consequence many blacks chose membership in the NMA by default and political necessity. Since desegregation, it seems reasonable to assume that membership of blacks in the AMA will have increased. Published information, however, needed to verify race or ethnic-related growth in its membership was difficult to obtain.

For the most part, published documents provided general information on numbers of physicians in the AMA, but without regard to race even as recently as the 1990 Census. Some publications, however, did show differentiation in AMA membership by gender. When I called the membership office of the AMA to determine if data on race or ethnicity of members could be released by special request (May 1997), I was advised that the AMA does not collect data on the racial identity of its members.

The National Medical Association as a Source of Professional and Personal Support for its Members

The NMA was more than a membership group for black physicians. The numbers of blacks who have held membership and/or who have identified with the group have varied over the decades since 1895 depending on a number of factors: (1) Whether or not it was more idealized to seek membership in the AMA even when blacks were rejected by that organization; (2) The intensity of exclusion of blacks by state and local medical associations; and (3) The comparative advantages believed to be associated with membership in the NAACP, the Urban League, or other political action groups that were believed to be more powerful and successful as advocates for black physicians.

As a foundation and reinforcer of self-esteem, especially between 1895 and 1965 when many blacks were excluded on the basis of race from the inner circles of the AMA; secondly, as a catalyst for improvements in the treatment of blacks in the profession of medicine; and finally, as a reinforcer of the importance of the mission to serve the poor and under-served, the NMA made a marked difference in the lives of many practicing black physicians and students who aspired to join the profession. The NMA has also actively engaged in efforts to expand access to medical education. Work in this area has included efforts to upgrade and sustain the highest quality educational standards in the handful of historically black medical schools in the United States and in the development of health careers programs in secondary schools and in undergraduate curriculae.

Members of the NMA have also been active in efforts to help shape national health care policy. They were among the strongest supporters of Congressional hearings and legislative developments leading to Medicaid, the major public source of health care for the poor since 1965. Further, many of its members were active advocates in recent years for national health care insurance, especially those parts of the Clinton proposal that would have extended coverage to all of the poor and underserved in the United States.

As a part of its efforts at continuing education for its members, the NMA has kept a close watch on recent developments in managed care organizations and encouraged discussions among its members about the bearing of managed care on doctor-patient relationships and the implications for the economic and professional futures of black physicians. There is further discussion of this topic later in this chapter. The efforts of the NMA as a watchdog on political and economic developments pertinent to national health care policy and as a collective advocate for black physicians and patients have probably been among its most important functions since 1895.

Race and Medical Education in the United States

Another indicator of desegregation is represented by student enrollment in institutions of medical education. In a study published in 1994 by the AMA Department of Data Services, it was reported that 670,336 physicians had been graduated by 1993 in the United States.[5] Of this number, 1.1 percent or 7557 were graduated by the Howard, Meharry, and Morehouse Schools of Medicine, all in the twentieth century. It should

TABLE 12.2
Production of Physicians by Historically Black Medical Schools
in the Twentieth Century

	Total Grads	Prior to 1940	1941–1949	1950–1959	1960–1969	1970–1979	1980–1989	1990–Present
Howard	4109	167	343	552	781	998	1043	223
Meharry	3243	111	331	453	505	827	847	169
Morehouse	205	—	—	—	—	—	122	82
Charles R. Drew post-grad School	Not listed	—	—	—	—	—	—	—
Total Blacks	7557	278	674	1005	1286	1825	2012	474
% Blacks	1.12	1.06	1.40	1.29	1.14	1.13	1.03	1.00
Total (all M.D.'s regardless of race or medical school)	670,336	25,983	48,088	77,844	112,729	161,187	195,813	48,712

Source: This table was constructed from data published in the following source. *Physician Characteristics and Distribution in the United States*, by Gene Roback, Lilian Randolph, Bradley Seidman, and Thomas Pasko (Washington, DC: American Medical Association, Department of Date Services, 1994, pp. 65–66).

be noted that the Charles R. Drew Post-Graduate Medical School was also recognized as an historically black medical school (founded in 1968), but reported no graduates by the time of the AMA study (see table 12.2).

With regard to the focus on black physicians and the prospect of accelerating the desegregation of medical education, table 12.2 shows a steady decline in the number of M.D.'s graduated by the historically black medical schools from 1950 through the mid-1990s. This finding, however, must be interpreted with caution. On the one hand, the declining percentages may indicate reductions in the production of M.D.'s by historically black schools relative to other medical schools in the United States since 1954. Since increasing numbers of historically segregated medical schools opened their doors to black students following the court and legislative decisions against segregation beginning in 1954, many black students who availed themselves of these new educational opportunities would not have shown up among HBCU (historically black colleges and universities) graduates.

Alternatively, the declining percentage of graduates from black medical schools between 1950 and the mid-1990s may have been a function of growth in the absolute numbers of M.D.'s produced by all medical schools in relation to which enrollments at the historically black medical schools may have been relatively static, showing little or no significant increases in the production of M.D.'s since mid-century. This latter hypothesis suggests that the declining percentages of graduates from historically black medical schools may be a statistical artifact, reflecting flux in relation to growth in the overall volume of medical school enrollees, a changing baseline as it were, including women; not a substantial decline in graduates from historically black medical schools since the 1950s.

In 1970, the Association of American Medical Colleges (AAMC) found that only 2.8 percent of all students enrolled in medical schools were black.[6] In the same year, the AAMC developed a strategy to remove barriers and increase access to the medical profession for blacks. The short range goal was to increase the proportion of minority students from 2.8 percent to 12 percent by 1976. By 1976, however, minority enrollment had reached only 8.2 percent of the total[7] and leveled off for the next ten years. The reasons for the plateau were not clear, but some hypotheses can be suggested. One factor that may have played a part was the public protest over the allegation of "lowered admissions standards" used at some medical schools to help reach the minority enrollment goals. It was argued that lowering the admissions standards would lead to the production of "inferior" physicians and constitute "reverse discrimination," as well.[8] Two court cases and decisions, Defunis and Bakke, grew out of these contentions and led to a 1978 ruling of the California Supreme Court that lowering standards to favor minorities was unconstitutional.[9] These events left many medical school admissions committees uncertain about their previous interpretations of Affirmative Action Law and the implementation of programs at their institutions. In practice, at some institutions, the intensity of efforts to recruit minorities has shown signs of weakening since Bakke, but overall growth in minority enrollment has continued. For example, by 1992 the number of minorities entering medical school was 1,827 or 11.2 percent, the highest number recorded for any given year up to that date.[10]

The continuing growth in the enrollment of black and other minority students may have been related to the long range goals and efforts of the AAMC in "Project 3000 by 2000."[11] This project was intended, through various efforts, to increase the first year medical school enrollment of minorities to 3000 by the year 2000. While the number of black applicants had exceeded 3000 by 1996, with females outnumbering males, the number accepted was considerably below 3000. It should be noted that the enrollment of black females has shown steady growth since the mid 1970s, while the enrollment of black males has shown a gradual decline.[12] In addition to Project 3000 by 2000, three other factors may have played a part in the increased numbers of blacks who enrolled and completed medical school since 1970: (1) there was an increase in the number of medical school facilities, including the construction of the Morehouse School of Medicine that was opened in 1974 as a two year institution and then as a full four year program in 1978; (2) there was increased recruitment of black faculty at medical schools, including some that were previously segregated.[13] The increased representation of blacks among faculty made these medical schools more attractive to black and other minority students and symbolized another active role that blacks could play in the medical establishment upon completing their education; and , (3) there was growth in private and public emphases on health careers, including government programs, such as affirmative action. These emphases encouraged interest in science, health education, and related careers. In educational institutions, some interest groups focused on students as early as the high school years.[14] Further, some HBCU, added and/or expanded their existing health careers programs.

Distribution and Work Force Participation by Black Physicians

Over the decades, the places of work of physicians have been largely influenced by the changing patterns of migration and population densities of prospective patients in the locality where the physician considered establishing a practice. The general population of the United States was predominantly rural until the post-World War I period. By 1920, however, white Americans had become preponderantly urban; thirty years later, by 1950, black Americans had also become predominantly urban (see table 9.3).

The growing concentration of black physicians in urban areas along with the general population has continued since 1950, although not at the same rate of growth. As shown above, the general population of blacks grew from 8 percent in 1950 to 11 percent in 1970 and 12.3 percent in 1990. By contrast, the number of black physicians showed little growth, increasing from 1 to 4 percent during the same period (see tables 12.1 and 12.2).

Secondly, more than 60 percent of the black students enrolled in medical schools in 1970 were resident at the Howard University School of Medicine and the Meharry Medical College.[15] Large proportions of the graduates elected to practice in federally designated areas of poor and underserved people and/or in the state or town of the physician's origin.[16] Over the years, however, increasing numbers who were not already in the northern United States have moved northward after graduation to establish private practices and/or compete for staff positions

TABLE 12.3
Black Physicians by Selected Specialties in the Workforce, 1996

	Fi	%
Internal Medicine*	291	29.0
Family Practice	183	18.2
Surgery**	123	12.2
Pediatrics	123	12.2
Ob-Gyn	107	10.6
Transitional***	56	5.6
Emergency Medicine	42	4.2
Psychiatry	37	3.7
Pathology	11	1.1
Anesthessiology	6	0.6
Physical Med. & Rehab.	6	0.6
Radiology	5	0.5
Urology	4	0.4
Otolaryngology	4	0.4
Preventive Medicine	3	0.3
Neurology	2	0.2
Ophthalmology	1	0.1
Dermatology	1	0.1
	N= 1005	100.0

Source: This table is based upon raw data published in the "Census of Graduate Medical Education." *Minority Students in Medical Education: Facts and Figures*, vol. 10 (Washington, DC: Association of American Medical Colleges, 1997, pp. 90–91, tables 21a and 21b).

*This specialty subsumes general as well as preliminary, primary care, and pediatric internal medicine.
**This specialty subsumes general as well as orthopedic, neurologic, oral, and preliminary surgery.
***This category refers to practitioners who were uncertain about their choice of a specialty.

and privileges in one or more of the newly desegregated hospitals or medical centers.

While the numbers have increased and social integration has improved, a 1990 survey suggested that by area of specialization in the work force, black physicians were still primarily general practicioners.[17] By 1996, however, blacks had begun to show much greater representation among the specialties in medicine. Table 12.3 shows the distribution of specialties among black physicians in the work force as represented by a 1996 sample of blacks published by the AAMC . It should be noted, in table 12.3 that more than 60 percent of the physicians reporting listed specialties in internal medicine, family practice, and surgery.

Another recent survey shows that a growing number of blacks, since 1970, in their first year of medical school chose osteopathic over allopathic courses of study.[18] This pattern may be related to a growing interest in holistic approaches to health care. While first year enrollment in schools of osteopathic medicine tripled between 1971–1972 and 1987–1988, regardless of race and ethnicity of the student, first-year enrollment of black and other minority students increased tenfold during the same periods, from 2.4 percent to 6.2 percent of total first year enrollment.[19]

Osteopathy is based on the theory that the body is capable of making its own remedies against disease and other toxic conditions when it is in normal structural relationship and has favorable environmental conditions and adequate nutrition. It utilizes generally accepted physical medicinal and surgical methods of diagnosis and therapy, while placing chief emphasis on the importance of normal body mechanics and manipulative methods of detecting and correcting faulty structures.[20]

The focus on environmental and nutritional factors links osteopathy with a number of alternative medical approaches to health care and their emphases on holistic perspectives.[21] It should be also noted that the Bureau of Health Professions of the U.S. Public Health Service projects that accelerated enrollment of minorities in schools of osteopathic medicine will probably continue at least through the year 2010.[22]

Regardless of their specialties, contemporary black physicians have become major providers of health care services for the poor and underserved.[23] This outcome is not surprising, consistent as it is with the historical interests of black physicians and the affirmative action emphases on the recruitment of minority enrollees for medical schools and the postgraduate service agreements that their enrollments implied.[24]

TABLE 12.4

**Percentage of Patients Treated in Each Racial or Ethnic Group,
according to Race or Ethnic Group of Physician in the year 1975***

Race/Ethnic Group of Patients	Race/Ethnic Group of Physician				
	Black	Hispanic	American Indian	Asian	White
Black	56.4**	8.4	13.0	10.6	13.7
Hispanic	7.6	30.1**	9.4	9.3	6.1
American Indian	0.5	1.0	7.9**	0.6	1.3
Asian	2.4	2.6	2.5	15.9**	2.3
White	32.9	57.0	67.1	63.6	76.5**
All races	100.0	100.0	100.0	100.0	100.0
Sample size	349	64	27	42	1199

*Table excludes physicians who are not in direct patient care.
**The average percentage of patients from the same ethnic or racial group as each physician group (e.g. black patients of black physicians) is consistently higher than the percentage of patients treated by physicians of different ethnic groups (e.g. black patients of white physicians, black patients of Hispanic physicians). These differences are statistically significant (P<0.001 as assessed by two-sample t-test).

Source: Stephen N. Keith, Robert N. Ball, August G. Swanson and Albert P. Williams, Affects of Affirmative Action in Medical Schools. New England Journal of Medicine. 313 (1985): 1519–1525.

Black Physicians and Their Patients

Partly as a result of the requirements of affirmative action programs and the emphases on increasing the quantity and quality of health care services for the poor and underserved, who were disproportionately black Americans, the patient loads of many contemporary black physicians are still preponderantly black (see table 12.4), although not for the same reasons that prevailed before affirmative action.

The concentration of black patients with black physicians was not as intense in 1975 as it was before the inception of the legal and social forces that compelled widespread desegregation after 1954. Nevertheless, the current distribution of patients by ethnicity, matched with that of their physician's continues to mirror the pre-1954 pattern documented earlier in this study.

It should be noted that table 12.4 also suggests signs of ethnic integration within the medical market place. For example, the patients of the minority physicians were categorically similar to those of their non-minority counterparts, although not in the same proportions. Other indicators of social integration, especially in medical centers, is the growing tolerance of white physicians shown toward blacks as staff colleagues and the numbers of staff positions awarded blacks in previously all-white medical centers. Some research suggests that these concessions to black physicians have in many places been yielded grudgingly. For example, non-technical factors, such as personality and social background were heavily weighted by some established white physicians; they did not want new members on staff who threatened to rock the boat.[25] Secondly, where blacks obtained appointments in previously segregated medical centers, most were assigned to low status positions with little power and responsibility.[26] For previous discussions of black physicians and hospital staff development, see chapters 4, 6,7,9 and 10.

Socioeconomic Class and the Challenge of Expanding Medical Services to the Poor and Underserved

The development of blacks in medicine has been accompanied by a concern among them that they be able to achieve through their practices of medicine reasonable economic returns on their educational and professional investments.[27] With the increasing costs of medical education, malpractice insurance, and establishing private practices, these economic questions have become more pressing in recent years. Seeking well-insured and fee-for-service patients, developing relatively large but manageable patient loads and carefully selecting one or more locations for private practices were among the means by which physicians have sought to achieve their economic goals.[28]

Before 1954, black physicians when compared to whites had limited economic successes through their private practices because most of their patients were poor and did not have comprehensive health insurance options (see chapter 5 for a previous discussion of this topic). For many, the only means of compensating for the low returns from their low-income patients was the recruitment of large numbers who often had to queue for services for hours in small overcrowded waiting rooms. For the most part, before and since the mid-century movements toward desegregation, black physicians have been disproportionately represented in services to the black, the poor, and uninsured and/or underinsured patients living in racially and/or ethnically segregated ghettoes.[29] Ironically, while the Supreme Court decisions of 1954 and the 1965 revisions of the Hill-Burton Act helped to shatter the walls of segregation and reverse major legal barriers to the professional and economic mobility of black physicians and other professionals, the affirmative action mandates of the 1970s introduced new constraints on the prospective economic successes of black physicians. In particular, the public expectation that beneficiaries of affirmative action interventions will participate in extending health services to the poor and underserved foretold a risk that large numbers of black physicians would continue to realize lower returns on their investments in medical education and practice when compared to their white counterparts.[30]

It is already conceded that desegregation has opened new opportunities for the professional growth of black physicians. Gaining staff positions in highly technological and previously all-white medical centers has facilitated the development of specialties in previously restricted areas, such as surgery, and increases in income for the few who have transgressed these barriers. These kinds of successes, however, do not represent the majority of black physicians.

With the advent of Medicaid (1965), it is true that increased numbers of the poor and underserved gained access to health insurance designed in particular for the poor. The level of coverage, however, relative to fees for primary care is less than 30 to 50 percent of usual costs in some states.[31] In addition, the physician must at his/her own expense develop and maintain detailed records on each patient for whose costs the physician can make monthly claims on a cost-reimbursement basis.

In 1994, 9 million black Americans identified Medicaid as their primary source of health insurance and an estimated 7 million reported having no insurance of any kind.[32] More than likely, most members of these groups will be included among the poor and underserved and will be disproportionately represented among patients seen by black and other minority physicians for years to come. This pattern was already manifest for black and Hispanic physicians by 1975.[33] Clearly, increasing the quantity and quality of health services to the poor and underserved is important to the general health of the nation. This will be costly to all taxpayers as well as physicians and the variety of health-service delivery organizations. Currently, however, the major professional burden seems to have fallen upon black physicians. As members of a group who have been historically disadvantaged since their nineteenth century emergence in the profession of medicine, these post-desegregation developments are showing signs of discouraging some blacks from pursuing education and careers in medicine.[34] To add to their historical disadvantages and the challenges of desegregation are the social and economic changes in the organization of the profession induced by managed care organizations.

The Challenges of Managed Care

Currently, fewer blacks are covered by managed care plans than their white American counterparts. This is because blacks, on the average, have a lower base income, higher unemployment, and a greater percentage of uninsured persons.[35] Because the patients of black physicians are largely from among the poor and underserved, neither black patients nor black physicians are currently participating in managed care companies as much as their white American counterparts. Current trends, however, suggest that black Americans may soon outnumber whites in managed care plans because of the recently mandated participation of Medicaid populations in many states.[36] Nineteen states have already approved section 1915b of the Health Care Financing Administration's Waivers to establish or expand their Medicaid managed care programs; another seventeen states have waivers pending.[37]

Managed care means medical care delivered through a system that reduces costs by rationalizing or carefully regulating utilization.[38] Key to the implementation of managed care plans is the work of the primary care physician. It is the role of the primary care physician to ascertain in advance that the patient's access to specialized diagnostic and therapeutic services is commensurate, but not excessive, relative to the needs of the patient. This includes not using hospital admissions, excessive numbers of inpatient days, and/or expensive laboratory and other procedures except where those are clearly indicated. Cost containment while maintaining quality of care is key.

Challenges to the Status of Black Physicians
under Managed Care

In a recent survey of black physicians, 92 percent (n=305) claimed that they were treated less favorably than their white colleagues in managed care organizations.[39] For example, they claimed that their contracts with managed care organizations were terminated more often than those of their white counterparts, usually with no reason given. This finding needs to be investigated carefully through a larger comparative sample, including white and other minority physicians to determine if there are widespread patterns showing differential treatment of physicians by ethnicity, patient characteristics, admissions and discharge practices, and other factors. In spite of the claims of differential termination, 75 percent of the physicians in this survey said that their patient loads had either grown or remained the same.[40] This means that they had found the means to cope or, by default, were adjusting to the challenges brought by managed care organizations.

We previously showed that the patients of black physicians tend to be overwhelmingly black and poor. It has also been documented that because of the historical segregation of health services in the United States and the absence of health insurance for millions, many blacks have had infrequent visits to physicians and other providers. As a consequence, blacks are more likely to have chronic disorders and require long-term care when they finally come to the attention of a physician.[41] Because this is one of the categories of patients often tracked to black physicians through managed-care evaluation, this characteristic of their practices may make them less attractive to managed care organizations.[42]

Another factor is the large number of blacks who depend upon Medicaid. We have already shown that managed care organizations have not yet embraced Medicaid populations in every state. Yet, this is a population whose health care accounts for 29 percent of the income of black physicians in the United States.[43]

In terms of professional organization, many black physicians have solo practices whereas managed care organizations prefer group practices.[44] Some physicians have adjusted to this requirement by joining existing groups or by forming new group practices.

Another professional attribute of importance to many managed care organizations is board certification of the physician. Some black physicians are not board certified and do not routinely engage in activities, such as acquiring continuing medical education credits, which help to achieve board certification. These are three key professional attributes that help to make physicians attractive to managed care organizations.[45]

Bringing Medicaid under managed care will certainly mean the prospect of new support for the practices of black physicians. But it may also mean new competition for the economic returns that can come from serving the newly (or about-to-be) insured black patients, many of whom were and still are among the poor and underserved, and previously conceded (so it seemed) in large numbers to black physicians. With desegregation, however, and the economics of managed care, including the new entrepreneurial physicians and for-profit health provider organizations, access to and disproportionate control of the market of black patients may no longer be as straight forward as it once was for black physicians.

Conclusions

The sources and opportunities for medical education, workforce participation, and ethnic diversity of patients of black physicians suggest that desegregation and affirmative action programs have achieved some successes toward forging a more open society. The numbers of blacks graduating from medical schools has increased substantially since 1970 although the numbers still do not represent the proportion of blacks in the general population. Work toward this goal, spurred by Project 3000 of the AAMC goes on. A recent "report card on the physician workforce in the United States," however, suggests that it may be another fifty years before the proportion of black physicians achieves parity with the proportion in the general population.[46]

While there has been slow growth in their general numbers, there have been notable successes in producing more black physicians in the practice of primary care and other specialties where there were serious shortages. Recent research shows that minorities are selecting specialties in these shortage areas in greater proportions than their nonminority counterparts.

It is also true that contemporary black physicians, in the aggregate, tend to have ethnically diverse patient populations. Their primary clientele, however, are still predominately black. These patterns are similar to the practices observed before mid-century, but not necessarily for the same reasons. There is some concern in the literature that if increasing the production of black physicians continues to be associated with segregated medical practices, for example, blacks primarily serving blacks, this will contribute little to the affirmative action goal of social integration. The apparent preference for ethnic parity, however, shows up for physician-patient relationships in each of the largest ethnic groups in the United States: whites, blacks, and Hispanics. These apparent interpersonal preferences in doctor-patient relationships may be solidly grounded in cultural historical roots, such as religious-sacred understandings, imagined or real bonds of kinship and community having little to do with the profession of medicine. The goals of affirmative action were correct, to help reverse decades of thwarted educational and occupational opportunity based on race and gender, and to increase the number of minority physicians and health services to the poor and underserved. With these structural barriers removed, patients should be free to select any available and affordable health care provider, even if those choices are tempered by personal preferences for ethnic parity between the patient and provider.

After centuries of race-related segregation and oppression in the United States, the Supreme Court decision of 1954, the Civil Rights Acts of 1964 and 1965 and the affirmative action laws of the 1970s were major events for minorities and their sympathizers. While the general concern with social integration was understandable as a societal goal, it should not be confused with the societal need to improve health services to the poor and underserved. Clearly these goals are interactive, but social movements toward them may not occur at the same pace. The data summarized in this chapter show that in the field of medicine, advances have been made on both fronts and, in all likelihood, will continue over the coming years. Entitlements under Medicaid have helped make health care available to record numbers of poor persons since 1965, while affirmative action in medicine has helped to produce more physicians to deliver those services. The future is promising, even though events are not moving along as rapidly as some interest groups would like.

A major organizational change that will no doubt be a part of the future of health care delivery systems is managed care. This area of change in the medical establishment foretells many new challenges for black physicians, some of which are outlined in this chapter. Managed care can be conceived as a political and economic approach to the delivery of health services aimed at the regulation of professional providers, how and which patients get served and the containment of costs of service delivery.

The messages for black physicians are mixed: some physicians, as we have shown, will be at risk of being squeezed out of or facing diminished opportunities to participate in the economic returns anticipated as Medicaid is brought under managed care.[47] Yet, others see the potential for growth and economic gain through the formation of group practices, which are preferred by managed care companies; changing their hospital affiliations and admissions practices; and improving their credentials, such as board certifications and the acquisition of continuing medical education credits.[48] There is also a recognition expressed by recent presidents of the NMA of the need for increased political participation of black physicians aimed at influencing legislative decisions pertinent to the future of national health care policy.[49] These hypotheses pertaining to the future of managed care along with desegregation and the evolving open society that is the United States foretells multifaceted challenges for black physicians and society-at-large.

Notes

1. George E. Schwartz, "Educational Characteristics of Members of the National Medical Association." *Journal of Medical Education,* vol. 46 (July 1971), p. 599.
2. This estimate is based upon a quotation given to me by the membership office of the NMA, Washington, DC, 3 July 1997. In round numbers, this figure is identical to the estimated number of black physicians in the United States reported by the U. S. Bureau of Labor Statistics in 1990 (see table 12.1). It is questionable whether or not this estimate given by the NMA for 1997 is merely a public relations gesture versus an accurate count of the membership. Secondly, the membership office was not clear on the number of white physicians who had joined the NMA. Clearly, however, it seemed reasonable to conclude that membership in the NMA has grown substantially since 1970, although the actual numbers may be debatable.
3. Paul Starr, *The Social Transformation of American Medicine* (New York : Basic Books, 1982), pp. 168–177.
4. Ibid., p. 168.
5. Gene Roback, Lillian Randolph, Bradley Seidman, and Thomas Pasko, "Physician Characteristics and Distribution in the United States" (Washington, DC: American Medical Association, Department of Data Services, 1994), pp. 65–66.
6. Stephen N. Keith, Robert M. Bell, August G. Swanson, and Albert P. Williams, "Affects of Affirmative Action in Medical Schools," *New England Journal of Medicine*, vol. 313 (1985), pp. 1519–1525.
7. Ibid., pp. 1520–1521.
8. Ibid.
9. "Balancing the Scales of Opportunity: Ensuring Racial and Ethnic Diversity in the Health Professions" (Washington, DC: National Academy Press, 1994), p. 44.
10. Ibid., p. 12.
11. Association of American Medical Colleges, "Minority Students in Medical Education: Facts and Figures" (Washington, DC: AAMC, 1996), p. 146.
12. Ibid., p. 447.
13. "Balancing the Scales," p. 12.
14. Ibid., pp. 26–32.
15. Keith et al., "Affirmative Action."
16. Ibid.; see also "Balancing the Scales," p. 16.
17. Vivian Overton Sammons, *Blacks in Science and Medicine* (New York: Hemisphere Publishing Corporation, 1990).
18. "Estimates and Projections of Black and Hispanic Physicians, Dentists and Pharmacists to 2010" (Washington, DC: USDHHS, Public Health Service, HRSA, May, 1996), p. 40.
19. "Balancing the Scales," p. 36.

20. William Alexander Dorland, *Dorland's Illustrated Medical Dictionary,* 26th ed., (Philadelphia, PA: W.B. Saunders Company, 1985), p. 943.
21. Wilbur H. Watson, *Black Folk Medicine: The Therapeutic Significance of Faith and Trust* (New Brunswick, NJ: Transaction Publishers, 1984).
22. "Estimates and Projections," p. 40.
23. Keith et al., "Affirmative Action."
24. Ibid.
25. Starr, *Social Transformation,* pp. 167–168.
26. Ibid., p. 167.
27. Anthony R. Kovner (ed.), *Jona's Health Care Delivery in the United States,* 5th ed. (New York: Springer Publishing Company, 1995), p. 65.
28. Dana J. Selden, "Health Care Ethics," pp. 468–537 in Kovner, *Jona's Health Care Delivery* (see especially the discussion of "the two-tier system of health care," p. 503).
29. John C. Norman (ed.), *Medicine in the Ghetto* (New York: Alfred A. Knopf, 1968); see also Keith et al., "Affirmative Action."
30. Keith et al., "Affirmative Action."
31. Kovner, *Jona's Health Care Delivery,* pp. 132, 502.
32. "Statistical Abstract of the United States, 1996," *The National Data Book* (U.S. Department of Commerce, Economics and Statistical Administration, Bureau of the Census, October1996), p. 120, table 173.
33. Keith et al., "Affirmative Action."
34. Kovner, *Jona's Health Care Delivery,* p. 65.
35. Risa Lavizzo-Mourey, L.A. Clayton, W. M. Byrd, G. Johnson, III, and D. Richardson, "The Perceptions of African-American Physicians Concerning Their Treatment by Managed Care Organizations," *J.N.M.A.,* vol. 88, no. 4 (1996), p. 210.
36. Ibid.
37. Ibid.
38. Walter P. Lomax, "Medicaid Managed Care in Pennsylvania: The HMA Experience." *J.N.M.A.,* vol. 86, no. 6 (1994), p. 423.
39. Lavizzo-Mourey et al., "Perceptions," p. 213.
40. Ibid., pp. 211–212.
41. Ibid., p. 213.
42. Hobart C. Jackson, "Double Jeopardy," (New York: The National Urban League, 1964); also see Isabel Lindsay, "The Multiple Hazards of Age and Race," (Washington, DC: U.S. Government Printing Office, 1971).
43. Lavizzo-Mourey et al., "Perceptions," p. 213.
44. Ibid., p. 214.
45. Ibid.
46. Marc L. Rivo and David A. Kindig, "A Report Card on the Physician Work Force in the United States," *The New England Journal of Medicine,* vol. 334, no. 14 (4 April 1996), pp. 893 and 895.
47. Lomax, "Medicaid Managed Care," p. 424.
48. Ibid.; see also Lavizzo-Mourey et al., "Perceptions," pp. 210–214; Selden, "Health Care Ethics," pp. 503–504; and Randall C. Morgan, "Ethical Issues in Managed Care," *J.N.M.A.,* vol. 88, no. 8 (1996), pp. 479–480.
49. Yvonneris Smith Veal, "Wanted: A Few Committed African-American Physicians." *J.N.M.A..,* vol. 87, no. 8 (1995), pp. 529–530; Morgan, "Ethical Issues in Managed Care," pp. 479–480; and Ronald O. Butcher, "Managed Care Now and Forever," *J.N.M.A* , vol. 85, no. 7 (1993), pp. 505–507; see also Charles H. Wright, *The National Medical Association Demands Equal Opportunity : Nothing More, Nothing Less* (Southfield, MI: Charro Book Co., 1995).

13

Conclusions

> *There is no greater opportunity for brilliant achieve-*
> *ment, along all lines of public health work, than exists*
> *today in African American communities. Public*
> *opinion can and should be changed. There is a moral*
> *responsibility, not being assumed even for the white*
> *population, when the black people are neglected.*
> —Bousfield (1934)[1]

The practice of medicine by African American physicians in the United States was the focus of this study. Like the general history of blacks in the United States, the social structure of medical practice has been largely defined by patterns of racial segregation.

The historical period between 1896 and 1965 was of primary interest. The year 1896 marked the *Plessy v. Ferguson* decision that ushered in a fifty-eight-year period of juridically sanctioned separation of public accommodations for blacks and whites. That 1896 landmark decision was not reversed until 1954 through the Supreme Court decision on *Brown v. the Board of Education of Topeka, Kansas*. In that decision the Court declared that racially separate public schools, and by extension, other racially segregated public facilities, were inherently unconstitutional.

With respect to the significance of access to hospitals, the 1954 Supreme Court decision was less decisive for black physicians than the 1965 amendments to the Hill-Burton Act. The latter amendment prohibited further use of public monies for the construction and operation of racially segregated hospitals.

Since 1965 black physicians have made major inroads in acquiring staff positions at previously all-white hospitals. Secondly, desegregation of hospital wards paved the way for black physicians to admit black patients, without a white sponsor, to previously segregated hospitals.

The Underdevelopment of Medical Professionals and Health Care Delivery Systems for African Americans

Part I described and developed interpretations of various events related to the broad social and cultural history of African American development in the profession of medicine. The discussion showed the pervasiveness of the color line in institutions associated with the development of professional personnel and health care delivery in the United States.

While there were noteworthy developments in the formulation of institutional means for African Americans to establish health care intervention systems, there were also tremendous obstacles to achieving those goals. The founding of the Freedmen's Hospital in 1866 and the Howard University School of Medicine in 1869 followed by Meharry Medical College in 1876 were milestones in the efforts to increase the production of African American physicians. Moreover, eight additional medical colleges and/or departments intended to contribute to the production of African American physicians were developed between 1876 and 1900. Yet, as shown in chapter 2, the results were mixed. Some of these institutions graduated hundreds of students, others spawned no graduates at all. The quality of facilities and faculty for medical education ranged from excellent to poor.

By 1920, only the Howard University School of Medicine and the Meharry Medical College were still operating. Much later in the twentieth century the Drew Post Graduate Medical School (1968) and the Morehouse School of Medicine (1978) opened their doors and began contributing to this class of professionals.

It is noteworthy and not previously documented in a single source, that six of the ten institutions for medical education for blacks were in the state of Tennessee. The research yielded no conclusive explanation for this finding. Several hypotheses, however, are set for in chapter 2.

For at least a century, starting in 1850, medical college admissions boards were dominated by men in the United States. Until the midtwentieth century there were also pervasive biases that women who sought medical education were or should be looked upon askance. These biases were related to the belief that the proper place for women was in the home or in other settings favorable to domestic skills. Secondly, it was widely believed that so far as women may be admitted to institutions of higher education, they should not be admitted to classes with men. While a trickle of women succeeded in gaining access to medical schools and establishing medical practices by the mid-nineteenth century, African American women were but a small fraction among them.

In addition to sexist biases expressed by men against women in medicine, the African American woman was confronted by the color line. The duality of these factors obstructed access to medical education and practice, and helped to limit the kinds of specialties that came to characterize the preponderance of African American women in medicine. Many women were guided or cajoled into specialties in pediatrics and gynecology, specialties for which "their character was suited," according to some male observers. Seldom, however, until the affirmative action period (1972–present) were increases noted in the development of women physicians in surgery and other specialties previously dominated by men.

In spite of discrimination against women in their attempts to gain access to medical education and practice, many women made important contributions as "medical missionaries" in South Central Africa and in the development of community health services for the poor in the United States. Important contributions were also made to nursing education, hospital development, and health administration. In fact, some women health professionals, not necessarily medical doctors, during the first half of the twentieth century controlled the only hospital facilities in some localities, such as Georgetown, South Carolina, whose beds served the interests of blacks and whites, physicians and patients alike.

Chapter 4 also shows that the rise of black owned and operated hospitals was closely associated with the intensification of racial separatism following the year 1896, but declined sharply after passage of the amended Hill-Burton Act of 1965. With the exception of the Howard University Hospital (formerly the Freedmen's Hospital) and the hospital of the Veterans Administration Medical Center in Tuskegee, Alabama, most of the hospitals associated with medical centers where many black physicians completed residencies have either closed their doors, or merged since 1965 with predominantly white facilities.

As research has shown in the histories of health care in other ethnic groups, health beliefs and historical customs, such as uses of folk medicines in health care intervention were significant features in the cultural development of African Americans in biomedicine. Chapters 4, 7, and 10 discussed the roles and influences of folk practitioners as inter-mediaries between patients and physicians by, for example, being sought for "lay diagnoses" of putative "disorders" to determine whether or not help by another professional was needed. The discussion also shows the co-participation of some folk practitioners, such as rural midwives with physicians in the delivery of infants through small infirmaries and public health clinics. This kind of cooperation was not evident in all localities. It was sufficiently widespread, however to show the extent to which physicians and lay professional health care providers could, and often did, put aside their pride about differences in kinds and de-grees of professional training and extend their willingness to cooperate to achieve improvements in health care for anyone in need.

Access to Health Care Services

Following upon the broad social historical and political develop-ments in medicine as set forth in part 1, the focus in part 2 concentrated on a variety of microsociological questions about race and social status in the structure of help-seeking behavior. Secondly, careful attention was given social psychological factors in the practice of medicine, such as doctor-patient relationships.

Pathways to health care facilities and providers are often more con-voluted than the nondiscerning eye can see. Although physical pain, broken limbs, emotional disorders, or other maladies are often among the precipitating factors motivating individuals to seek professional help, those forces in themselves are usually not sufficient to achieve the ac-quisition of professional health care services. There is a myriad of in-termediate factors normally standing between the person in need and the prospective health care provider. These factors, such as when to schedule an appointment, and determining how payment will be made for the desired services are normally negotiated before the consump-tion of services. Furthermore, getting the impaired person to the health care provider means the need for transportation. This task, transporta-tion, is simplified when the health care provider, such as a midwife, is a member of the same family, kinship group or neighborhood as the prospective patient. Similarly, a physician or an alternative healer, like the old "country doctor," who lives in or near a neighborhood or small town where he or she also has a private practice helps to minimize transportation problems. Rural folk practitioners and neighborhood based physicians, although not necessarily black, were widespread among African Americans between the late nineteenth and the mid-twentieth century United States. As shown in chapter 7 on "Doctor Shopping" and in chapter 9 on "The Country Doctor," the absence of African American physicians in some localities meant that black people often turned to white physicians, although the shortage of black physicians was not the sole reason for the selection of white physicians by blacks. Clearly, however, the greater the distance between the impaired person and the service provider, the more crucial and sometimes more difficult it was to solve the problem of transportation. The result was often a failure to acquire needed health care.

Medicaid

Since the inception of Medicaid (1965) provisions under the Social Security Act of the United States, access to health care for the poor has improved considerably. With the disproportionate numbers of black families with children, along with older, poor blacks living below the poverty line, Medicaid has contributed to important advances in health care for the poor and underserved.[2] Consequently, black physicians with significant numbers of poor patients have benefited as well. On the other hand, as we showed in chapters 5, 7, and 12, most preferred fee-for-service patients, especially in regard to the low level of reimbursement through Medicaid relative to the actual costs of services.

Chapters 5 and 7 also showed the flexibility and tolerance of some black physicians in responses to patients who lacked the economic means to pay the costs of the services they required. Noteworthy was the willingness of some physicians to accept selected commodities and services in lieu of money in exchange for health care services. In addition to money and commodities as media of exchange, various forms of health insurance programs had begun to be developed by and for blacks early in the twentieth century, for example, the North Carolina Mutual Insurance Company and the Atlanta Life Insurance Companies were forerunners among private developers. Then with the passage of the Social Security Act of 1935 and other revisions and expansions of benefits under the Act in recent years, as noted above, public health insurance for the poor has made health care more accessible for more people. Yet some physicians refused to accept patients whose health care costs were paid by public assistance programs. Moreover, this study showed that while some physicians accepted poor patients supported by public assistance, such as Medicaid, some physicians segregated the treatment of the poor to selected times and days of the week. Moreover, there was segregation of patients within the waiting rooms of some doctors, putatively to protect the fee-for-service patients from mixing with the poor.

To gain access to services, the impaired African American person had to overcome some of the same obstacles against which black physicians had to struggle to become successful in their practices. The most common and deeply entrenched among these factors was the "color line." As this study has shown, the color line, in some instances provided a symbolic bridge between black physicians and patients, constituting a common ground on which they could stand against a common enemy. Yet, in other instances, the color line divided them. For example, "doctor shopping," as shown in chapters 7 and 8, sometimes incited animosities that motivated each to turn against the other.

Coping with the Forces of Oppressive Dominance

The color line was deeply embedded in the social customs of American society with no subgroup more victimized than black Americans. In spite of these outcomes, many black physicians found ways to withstand the attempts by their oppressors to stunt their developments in the profession of medicine. The coping techniques were many and varied.

Some black physicians succumbed to the beliefs and customs of the period by, for example, not accepting white patients, just as some white physicians refused to accept black patients. There was, however, no evidence of racially segregated waiting rooms in the practices of black physicians even when they accepted white patients. Other physicians were openly defiant against the customs of discriminating against blacks. Some sought to induce improvements for blacks through litigation against racially discriminatory laws and customs. Others tried firm, but diplomatic negotiations with white medical directors of hospitals to secure staff positions for black physicians. Some of the latter efforts were successful even before the 1965 amendments to the Hill-Burton Act. Then there were those who gave up the struggle in the southern United States, choosing instead to flee to one or another northern city for a fresh new start with expectations of less racial discrimination.

It was originally expected that family and kin, as well as church groups would function to some extent as sources of support for black physicians during the period of separatism. The research, however, showed that the family was cited by physicians less frequently than the church and various professional and political groups as sources of support. In other studies of blacks in the United States during the first half of the twentieth century, the church was identified also as a significant source of support in coping with the conditions of adversity.[3] Yet, it seemed reasonable to expect that the family of the physician would be an important source of nurturance especially for emotional stamina and the proactive psychological outlook so often needed to rise each day to face the degradation ceremonies and other challenges confronting blacks in the profession of medicine.

Finally, some, but not all black physicians joined the NMA. This association was actually founded in 1895, one year before the *Plessy v. Ferguson* decision, for the purposes of challenging racial segregation and discrimination against blacks and other obstacles to their career advancement in the profession of medicine. It has continued as a proactive organization with varying degrees of success through its efforts since 1895. Unfortunately, however, many older black physicians interviewed for this study admitted that they never accepted the NMA as an effective organization and, consequently, never joined. For many of the latter, admission to the AMA was an idealized goal, in spite of their rejection during the period of separatism.

Desegregation and Black Physicians in an Open Society

As pointed out earlier, the period of de jure separatism ended in 1954 with the U.S. Supreme court decision in the case of *Brown v. the Board of Education of Topeka, Kansas*. Secondly, the last major statutory road block to blacks in the practice of medicine was removed in 1965 with the amendments to the Hill-Burton Act. Although these changes in Supreme Court decisions and law were milestones in the long struggle to achieve equal rights for blacks, there are no illusions that equal rights have been achieved in practice. While the struggle for equality goes on, black physicians have increasingly turned their attention to other issues that affect all physicians, regardless of ethnicity.

For example, one of the outcomes of desegregation has been the increasing access of black physicians to staff positions in previously "white only" hospitals. Partly because of the long years and intensive efforts by some black physicians to acquire these prestigious positions, many blacks gradually abandoned the historically black hospitals when desegregation came. As observed by a former medical director of the now defunct (1986) Flint Goodridge Hospital of New Orleans, not only did old and new black physicians cease to covet staff positions in black hospitals, they ceased to refer their patients as well. With increasing numbers of empty beds, that has become the experience of many former "black only" hospitals since desegregation, the permanent closing and/ or merger of these institutions has been the outcome. Today, many of the major hospitals are closed, no longer providing patient care, opportunities for internships, and residencies for African Americans as they did during the period of separatism. Of those that have survived and continue to thrive, the Howard University Hospital, Washington, DC (formerly the Freedmen's Hospital), the Homer G. Phillips Hospital, St. Louis (formerly St. Louis Hospital no. 2), the hospital of the Veterans Administration Medical Center, Tuskegee (formerly the "Hospital for Sick and Injured Colored War Veterans"), are among the best known. In 1994 the Hubbard Hospital of Meharry Medical College closed its doors. Since then, the old Hubbard Hospital Building has been renovated and in November, 1997, became the new site of the relocated Metropolitan Nashville General Hospital. With the ongoing problems of racial discrimination against blacks in the United States today, the growing numbers among the poor and underserved who cannot afford adequate health care, and the absence of a national health care policy, it remains to be seen whether or not the loss of black owned and operated hospitals will cost—in quality of health care and life—more than it has benefited African American people.

Health Insurance Costs and Managed Care Programs

Coincidental with social movements toward desegregation has been a growing emphasis on managed care especially with regard to cost containment for third-party insurers. One of the important features of managed care plans, developed since the mid-1980s has been provider discounts on the costs of health care services.[4] While employers have been major procurers of health plans affecting nearly half of the entire U.S. population, hospitals and physicians are among the major providers of health care. Clearly, employers are important customers of insurers and health planners. It is also true that insurers are attentive to the interests of providers.[5] For example, provider discounts on services have given insurers incentives to provide greater volumes of patients to cooperating hospitals, physicians, and other providers over their competitors. These kinds of arrangements, over time, have lead the way to various kinds of PPOs and other kinds of managed care programs.[6]

The development of managed care programs have been problematic for black physicians and hospitals for several reasons: first, many black physicians have had heavy loads of poor patients, some fully dependent upon Medicaid with its low cost-reimbursement ratios. As a consequence, these physicians could not afford to give discounts and remain competitive in private practice, considering malpractice insurance and all other costs that concern them. Secondly, because of developmental deficits in health care, many black patients are seriously and/or chronically impaired by the time they come to the attention of a physician, usually black, making the physician less attractive as a preferred provider. Third, even before the inception of managed care programs, many historically black hospitals had become decreasingly competitive as providers since the desegregation of the health care industries. With declining patient populations, and meager staff and technological resources, few black hospitals could afford to discount the costs of their services to compete with their well funded mainstream counterparts. As a result of a disproportionate supply of poor patients, and declining selections as preferred providers by insurers, the financial underpinnings have been increasingly removed from many historically black hospitals and staff physicians. Today, as shown in chapter 4, most of the historically black hospitals founded during the period of separatism have been forced to close their doors.

Ethics

Ethical issues about the rights of human subjects in medical research, uses of life support systems, and controversies about the right to life are also among major topics of the day. The physicians interviewed for this study seemed agreed that while some research on human subjects is needed to determine the courses of physical, mental, and emotional disorders and the effectiveness of alternative interventions, careful measures must be developed and implemented to protect the rights of human subjects. For example, of the few black physicians in this study who had detailed knowledge of the Tuskegee syphilis experiments, all were in agreement that the major flaw of the physicians of the United States Public Health Service who were responsible for the study was their failure to: (1) properly inform the subjects about the health risks that they took and to (2) offer those subjects the option of medical treatment (penicillin) when that became available early in the 1940s. As is well known today, all of the subjects in the Tuskegee syphilis experiments were African American males. All indications are that the unethical treatment of these subjects, beginning in the 1930s, was a continuing expression of deeply entrenched practices of discrimination against black Americans based, in part, upon the belief that they were "less than human" and did not warrant the unabridged protection that the United States government provided other citizens.

On the matter of life support systems, there seemed to be general agreement that these techniques should be used as part of treatment so far as there was the prospect of returning a person to a fully functioning being. There also seemed, however, to be consensus that life support systems should not be used merely to sustain an individual in a state of vegetation.

In regard to the "right to life," the physicians were generally in agreement that abortion is a matter that should be a result of an accord reached between doctor and patient. Secondly, it was also agreed that it was appropriate for the mother to take into account the kind of world that the child may be brought into and the quality of life that she or her family could provide.

Finally, part 3 includes a discussion of the historical place and decline of the country doctor, a physician who was primarily defined by a small office practice and frequent uses of house calls as a means of delivering health care services. These were primary tools of early black physicians from the mid-nineteenth century through the mid-twentieth century in many localities of the United States. In some rural areas, some small towns and inner-city neighborhoods, these customs can still be observed. It has been the growing urbanization of the population of the United States and centralization of medical care, largely defined by centers of health care organized around several specialized hospitals and clinics, that have contributed significantly to the declining presence of country doctors.

Perhaps inescapable as a legacy of the racially segmented and stratified society that was set in motion during slavery, and protracted through the next three centuries, the black business and professional classes now face a dilemma. On the one hand, it is widely agreed, especially among African Americans, that race related barriers to social and economic mobility have been deeply entrenched in the United States, although waning in the last half of the twentieth century. These kinds of barriers have been objects of persistent criticism by many blacks on moral, political, and economic grounds-setting limits, as they have on the levels of growth and improvements in the quality of life of African-

Americans.[7] Yet, as pointed out by a number of older physicians interviewed for this study, African-American entrepreneurs, politicians, and other advocates for social change must be careful during this current period of desegregation about indiscriminately sharing power and control of organizations developed by blacks during the pre-1965 period of de jure and de facto racial segregation. For example, in the development and management of integrated hospitals and colleges, prematurely relinquishing and/or sharing power may risk losing what opportunities blacks have (or may have had) to shape long-range changes in social policy and practices, including medical education and the practice, thereof. On the other hand, given the politically and economically competitive forces operating in the United States, including managed care, these may be moot questions. The preconditions of choice for black physicians, collective political and economic strength, may well have already been eroded by the wavering support for such groups as the NMA, on the one hand, and the grinding pressures of outside political and capitalistic interest groups, such as the AMA and managed care organizations in the United States. The economics of desegregation and managed care organizations clearly foretell the development of new challenges, along with the color line, with which black physicians must contend in the twenty-first century.

Notes

1. M. O. Bousfield, "Reaching the Negro Community," *Journal of Public Health*, vol. 24, no. 24 (1934), pp. 209–214.
2. Barbara Lyons, Diane Rowland, and Kristina Hanson, "Another Look at Medicaid," *Generations: Journal of the American Society on Aging*, vol. 20, no. 2 (Summer 1996), pp. 24–30.
3. E. Franklin Frazier, *The Negro Church in America* (New York: Schocken, 1974); see also C. Eric Lincoln, *The Black Muslims in America* (Boston, 1973).
4. Robert B. Friedland, "Managed Care and All of Us: The Role of Managed Care in the Future." *Generations: Journal of the American Society on Aging*, vol. 20, no. 2 (Summer 1996), p. 38.
5. Ibid., p. 37.
6. Ibid., p. 38. For a detailed discussion of the broad political and economic events giving rise to managed care, see Paul Starr, *The Social Transformation of American Medicine* (New York: Basic Books, 1982).
7. Manning Marable, *How Capitalism Underdeveloped Black America* (Boston: South End Press, 1983); see also Bart Landry, *The New Black Middle Class* (Berkeley and Los Angeles, CA: University of California Press, 1988); Na'im Akbar, *Breaking Chains of Psychological Slavery* (Tallahassee, FL: Mind Productions and Associates, 1996); Francis Cress Welsing, *The Isis Papers: The Keys to the Colors* (Chicago: Third World Press, 1991).

Key Archives and Physician Interviews

A study, such as this, requiring detailed historical records could not have been completed without the availability and access to numerous archives and other carefully preserved and managed library resources. Secondly, the professional history interviews provided by older black physicians who started their practices before desegregation were invaluable. This appendix includes a list of the archives, archivists and older black physicians who provided crucial support and insights pertinent to this study.

Archives	Institutions
MCP Archives, Black Women Physicians	Medical College of Pennsylvania, Philadelphia, PA Archivist: Margaret Jerrido
Learning Resources Center	Meharry Medical College, Nashville, TN Archivist: Mary McHollin
Knoxville College Archive	Knoxville College, Knoxville, TN
Moreland-Spingarn Collection	Howard University, Washington, DC
The Negro Collection	The Atlanta University Center Woodruff Library, Atlanta, GA Archivist: Minnie Clayton
The History Department	Main Branch, Cleveland Public Library, Cleveland, OH
The Booker T. Washington Collection	Tuskegee University, Tuskegee, AL
The Amistad Research Center	Formerly located at the Old Mint, New Orleans, LA(1985) Archivist: Florence Borders

Archives	Institutions
The Amistad Research Center	Currently located at Tulane University, New Orleans, LA
Special Collections	Shaw University, Durham, NC
History Department	Main Branch, Public Library, Mobile, AL
Schomberg Collection	Main Branch, New York Public Library, NY
Special Collections	Temple University, Philadelphia, PA
Special Collections	Harvard University Library, Cambridge, MA
Health Sciences Library	Emory University, Atlanta, GA
History Department	Voorhees College Library, Denmark, SC

African-American Physicians Who Permitted Me Interviews of Their Professional Histories

Alabama
   E. B. Goode (M.D.). Mobile, 6 May 1986
   O.S. Gumbs (M.D.). Mobile, 30 May 1986
   Howard Kenny, Jr. (M.D.). Tuskeegee, 12 March 1986
   J.W. Williams (M.D.). Tuskegee, 12 March 1986*

Georgia
   Frederick Funderberg (M.D.). Atlanta, 1 November 1985
   Nelson Mcghee, Jr. (M.D.). Atlanta, 20 October 1985

Louisiana
   William Adams (M.D.). New Orleans, 5–6 February 1986*
   Elbert E. Allen (M.D.). Shreveport, 28 January 1986*
   Jean Briere (M.D.). Shreveport, 29 January 1986
   Anthony Hackett (M.D.). New Orleans, 30 May 1986
   C. C. Haydell (M.D.). New Orleans, 3 February 1986*
   George Thomas (M.D.). New Orleans, 15 February 1986

Mississippi
   Nobel Frisby (M.D.). Greenville, 8 February 1986
   Matthew Page (M.D.). Greenville, 8 February 1986
   Lenwood Rayford (M.D.). Grenada, March 2, 1979.
   James Yeldell (M.D.). Greenville, 8 February 1986

North Carolina
William Alexander Cleland (M.D.). Durham, 6 June 1986
Hubert A. Eaton (M.D.). Wilmington, 1 May 1986
Leroy Swift (M.D.). Durham, 27 March 1986
Leroy W. Upperman (M.D.). Durham, 2 May 1986
Charles Watts (M.D.). Durham, 28 March 1986

South Carolina
Cornelius Johnathon Beck (M.D.). Georgetown, 22 March 1986
Joseph I. Hoffman (M.D.). Charleston, 21 March 1986
Turner McCottry (M.D.). Charleston, 23 March 1986
H. D. Monteith (M.D.). Columbia, 20 March 1986
Charles Stephenson (M.D.). Columbia, 19 March 1986

Virginia
William T. Forrester (M.D.). Richmond, 19 May 1986
Maurice Frazier (M.D.). Hampton, 21 May 1986
Joseph J.Quarles (M.D.). Norfolk, 13 May 1986
Margaret Reid (M.D.). Suffolk, 17 April 1986
L.T. Reid (M.D.). Suffolk, 15 May 1986
C. Waldo Scott (M.D.). Newport News, 14 May 1986
John Selden (M.D.). Norfolk, May 21, 1986
Everett C. White (M.D.). Richmond, 19 May 1986

Texas
Isadore J. Lamonte, Jr. (M.D.). Marshall, 28 January 1986

---

*No permission granted to quote from interview protocol.

References

Akbar, Na'im. 1996. *Breaking Chains of Psychological Slavery.* Tallahassee, FL : Mind Productions and Associates.

Association of American Medical Colleges. 1996. *Minority Students in Medical Education: Facts and Figures.* Washington, DC: AAMC.

Balancing the Scales of Opportunity: Ensuring Ethnic and Racial Diversity in the Health Professions. 1994. Washington, DC: National Academy Press.

Bateson, Gregory. 1960. "Minimal Requirements for a Theory of Schizophrenia." *Archives of General Psychiatry* 2: 477–94.

Beardsley, E.H. 1983. "Making Separate Equal: Black Physicians and the Problems of Medical Segregation in the Pre-World War II South." *Bulletin of the History of Medicine* 57 (Fall): 382–96.

———. 1983. "Dedicated Servant or Errant Professional: The Southern Negro Physician before World War II," pp. 142–167 in Walter Fraser, Jr. and Winfred B. Moore, Jr. (eds.), *The Southern Enigma: Essays on Race, Class and Folk Culture.* Westport, CT: Greenwood Press.

Bousfield, M. O. 1934."Reaching the Negro Community." *Journal of Public Health* 24: 209–214.

Bourg, Carroll J. 1971. "A Social Profile of Black Aged in a Southern Metropolitan Area," pp. 97–106 in J.J. Jackson (ed.), *Research Conference on Minority Group Aged in the South.* Durham, NC: Duke University Center for the Study of Aging.

Brooks, Charles H. 1973. "Association among Distance, Patient Satisfaction, and Utilization of Two Types of Inner City Clinics." *Medical Care* 11: 373–83.

Brown, Bertram Wyatt. 1982. *Southern Honor: Ethics and Behavior in the Old South.* New York: Oxford University Press.

Brown, Sara W. 1923. "Colored Women Physicians." *The Southern Workman* 52 (12): 580–593.

Butler, John Sibley. 1991. "Entrepreneurship and Self-Help among Black Americans." Albany, NY: State University of New York Press.

Caldwell, A.B. 1919. *History of the American Negro* (South Carolina ed.) Atlanta, GA: A.B. Caldwell Publishing Company.

Carter, Wilmoth A. 1973. *Shaw's Universe: A Monument to Educational Innovation.* Rockville, MD: D.C. National Publishing, Inc.

Cartwright, Joseph H. 1976. *The Triumph of Jim Crow: Tennessee Race Relations in the 1880s.* Knoxville, TN: The University of Tennessee Press.

Cobb, W. Montague. 1948. "Progress and Portents for the Negro in Medicine." *The Crisis* 55 (4): 107–122.

———. 1981. "Delaney the Redoubtable." *Journal of the National Medical Association* 73 (suppl.): 1205–1208.

———. 1981. "James McCune Smith: First Black American MD." *Journal of the National Medical Association* 73 (suppl.): 1205.

———. 1981. "The Black Physician in Medicine." *Journal of the National Medical Association* 73 (suppl.): 1185–1249.

———. 1981. "The Black American in Medicine." *Journal of the National Medical Association* 73 (suppl.): 1209.

———. 1981. "Holmes and Harvard." *Journal of the National Medical Association* 73 (suppl. 1981): 1205–1208.

Colby, Irac. 1985 . "The Freedmen's Bureau: From Social Welfare to Segregation." *Phylon* 46 (3): 228.

Curran, William J. 1984. "A Further Solution to the Malpractice Problem: Corporate Liability and Risk Management in Hospitals." *The New England Journal of Medicine* 310 (11): 704–705.

Curtis, James L. 1971. *Blacks, Medical Schools and Society*. Ann Arbor, MI: University of Michigan Press.

Davis, Allison, Burleigh B. Gardner, and Mary B. Gardner. 1965. *Deep South: A Social Anthropological Study of Castle and Class*. Chicago: Phoenix.

Davis, Milton S. 1985. "Attitudinal and Behavioral Aspects of the Doctor-Patient Relationship as Expressed and Exhibited by Medical Students and Their Mentors." *Journal of Medical Education* 43: 337–43.

Dawes, Robyn M., and Tom L. Smith. 1985. "Attitude and Opinion Measurement," pp. 509–566. in Gardner Lindzey and Elliott Aronson (eds.), *The Handbook of Social Psychology*, 3d ed., vol. 1). New York: Random House.

Delaney, Martin Robison. 1969. *The Condition, Elevation, Emigration, and Destiny of the Colored People of the United States*. New York: Arno Press and the *New York Times*.

Dorland, William Alexander. 1985. *Dorland's Illustrated Medical Dictionary* (26th ed.). Philadelphia, PA: W. B. Saunders Company.

Drake, St. Clair and Horace Cayton. 1987. *Black Metropolis*. Chicago: University of Chicago Press.

Dubois, W.E.B. 1961. *Souls of Black Folk*. New York: Fawcett Publications.

———. 1946. "The Future and Function of the Private Negro College." *The Crisis* 53 (Aug.): 234–46, 253–54.

———. 1973. *The Education of Black People: Ten Critiques, 1906–1960*, ed. Herbert Aptheker. Amherst, MA: University of Massachusetts Press, pp. 139–148.

Duffy, John, ed. 1962. *The Rudolph Matas History of Medicine in Louisiana*, vol. 2. Baton Rouge, LA: Louisiana State University Press.

"Early Black Women Physicians." *Women and Health* vol. 5, no. 3 (Fall 1980): 1.

Editorial. 1930. "Noted Physician and Surgeon, Humanitarian, Outstanding Citizen of Columbia." *The Palmetto Leader*, 22 March, pp. 1 and 8.

Editorial. 1933. "Can a Colored Woman Be a Physician?" *The Crisis Magazine* 40 (2): 33–34.

Estimates and Projections of Black and Hispanic Physicians, Dentists and Pharmicists to 2010. Washington, DC: USDHHS, Public Health Service, HRSA, May, 1996.

Fanon, Frantz. 1967. *Black Skin, White Masks*. New York: Grove Press.

Fisher, Walter. 1969. "Physicians and Slavery in the Antebellum Southern Medical Journal," pp. 153–164 in August Meier and Elliot Rudwick (eds.), *The Making of Black America*, Volume 1: *The Origins of Black Americans*. New York: Atheneum.

Flexner, Abraham. 1973. *Medical Education in the United States and Canada: A Report to the Carnegie Foundation*. New York: The Heritage Press.

Franklin, John Hope. 1989. *Race and History: Selected Essays, 1938–1988*. Baton Rouge, La: Louisiana State University Press.

Franklin, John Hope and Alfred A. Moss, Jr. 1994. *From Slavery to Freedom: A History of African Americans*. 7th ed. New York: McGraw-Hill.

Fraser, Jr., Walter and Winfred B. Moore, Jr.,eds. 1993. *The Southern Enigma: Essays on Race, Class and Folk Culture*. Westport, CT: Greenwood Press.

Frazier, E. Franklin. 1968. "Durham: Capitol of the Black Middle Class," pp. 333–340. in Alain Locke (ed.), *The New Negro*. New York: Atheneum.

———. 1974. *The Negro Church in America*. New York: Schocken.

Friedland, Robert B. 1996. "Managed Care and All of Us: The Role of Managed Care in the Future." *Generations: Journal of the American Society on Aging* 20 (2): 34–39.

Freidson, Eliot.1962. "Dilemmas in the Doctor-Patient Relationship," pp. 207–24 in Arnold M. Rose (ed.), *Human Behavior and Social Processes: An Interactionist Approach*. Boston: Houghton-Mifflin.

Freire, Paulo. 1970. *Pedagogy of the Oppressed*. New York: Herder and Herder.

Frost, J. William, ed. 1980. *The Quaker Origins of Antislavery*. Norwood, PA: Norwood Editions.

Gangitano, John B. 1972. "Health and the Low Income Family." *California Medicine* 116: 89–92.

Goffman, Erving. 1967. *Interaction Ritual: Essays in Face-to-Face Behavior*. Chicago: Aldine.

———. 1963. *Stigma: Notes on the Management of Spoiled Identity*. Englewood Cliffs, NJ: Prentice-Hall.

Goldenson, Robert M. 1970. *The Encyclopedia of Human Behavior,* vol.2. New York: Doubleday and Company, pp. 1162–1163.

Hamer, Philip M. 1930. *The Centennial History of the Tennessee State Medical Association*, 1830–1930. Nashville, TN.: Tennessee State Medical Association.

Harris, Joseph E., ed. 1982. *Global Dimensions of the African Diaspora*. Washington, DC: Howard University Press.

Harrison, Grace. 1945. Hubbard Hospital and Meharry Medical College for Negroes, Nashville, Tennessee (unpublished Masters Thesis, The University of Chicago), March.

Hersh, Blanche Glassman. 1979. "Am I Not a Woman and a Sister?" Abolitionist Beginnings of Nineteenth-Century Feminism," p. 252 in Lewis Perry and Michael Fellnam (eds.) *Antislavery Reconsidered: New Perspectives on the Abolitionist..* Baton Rouge, LA: Louisiana State University Press.

Herskovitz, Melville J. 1990. *The Myth of The Negro Past*. Boston: Beacon Press.

Higginbotham, A. Leon, Jr. 1978. *In the Matter of Color: Race and the American Legal Process / The Colonial Period*. New York: Oxford University Press.

Hill, M.C. and McCall, B.C. 1950. "Cracker Culture: A Preliminary Definition," *Phylon* 11 (3): 223–231.

Hine, Darlene Clark. 1985. "Co-Laborers in the Work of the Lord: Nineteenth-Century Black Women Physicians," pp. 107–120 in Ruth J. Abram (ed.) *Send Us a Lady Physician: Women Doctors in America*, 1835–1920. New York: W.W. Norton and Company.

———. 1984. "Health and The Afro-American Family." *Health*. Washington, DC: The Associated Publishers.

Hoentik, H. 1967. *Caribbean Race Relations: A Study of Two Variants,* translated from the Dutch by Eva M. Hooykaas. New York: Oxford University Press.

Holt, Emily. 1914. *Encyclopedia of Etiquette: A Book of Manners in Everyday Life*. New York: Doubleday, Page and Company.

Hubbard, G.W. 1900–01. "Dr. Georgia E. L. Patton Washington," *The Christian Educator* 12: 5.

Hunter, Gertrude, T. 1973. "Pediatrician." *Annals of the New York Academy of Sciences* 208 (March 15): 38–39.

Jaco, E. Gartley, ed. 1972. *Doctors, Patients, and Illness: A Sourcebook in Behavioral Science and Health*. New York: The Free Press.

Jackson, Hobart C. 1964. *Double Jeopardy*. New York.: The National Urban League.

Jay, William.[1838]1969. *Inquiry into the Character and Tendency of the American Colonization and American Anti-Slavery Societies*. New York: Negro Universities Press.

John A. Andrew Memorial Hospital Cares. 1975. Tuskegee Institute Alabama: Tuskegee Institute.

Johnson, Charles S. 1987. *Bitter Canaan: The Story of the Negro Republic,* with a new introduction by John Stanfield. New Brunswick, NJ: Transaction Publishers.

Jones, James H. 1993. *Bad Blood*. New York: The Free Press.

Kardiner, Abram and Lionel Ovesey. 1962. *The Mark of Oppression: Explorations in the Personality of the American Negro*. New York: Meridian Books.

Katzman, David M. 1973. *Before the Ghetto: Black Detroit in the Nineteenth Century*. Urbana, IL: University of Illinois Press.

Keith, Stephen N., Robert M. Bell, August G. Swanson, and Albert P. Williams. 1985."Affects of Affirmative Action in Medical Schools." *New England Journal of Medicine* 313: 1519–25.

Kimball, G.H. 1968–70. "Twentieth Century Fund," ç quoted in *The Biennial Report*, North Carolina Board of Health, p. 55.

King, Gary. 1980. "The Supply and Distribution of Black Physicians in the United States: 1900–1970." *Western Journal of Black Studies* 4 (1): 21–39.

Kovner, Anthony R., ed. 1995. *Jona's Health Care Delivery in the United States*. (5th ed.). New York: Springer Publishing Company.

Laidler, Percy Ward and Michael Gelfand. 1971. *South Africa/Its Medical History, 1652–1898: A Medical and Social Study*. Capetown: C. Struik (PTY) LTD.

Landry, Bart. 1988. *The New Black Middle Class*. Berkeley and Los Angeles, CA: University of California Press.

Lavizzo-Mourey, Risa, L. A. Clayton, W. M. Byrd, G. Johnson, III, and D. Richardson. 1996. "The Perceptions of African-American Physicians concerning Their Treatment by Managed Care Organizations." *J.N.M.A.* 88 (4): 210–214.

Lee, Anne S. 1987. "The Elderly in Black Belt Counties," in Wilbur H. Watson (ed.), *The Health of Older Blacks: Social and Demographic Factors*. Atlanta, GA: Center on Health and Aging of Atlanta University.

Lindsay, Inabel. 1971."Multiple Hazards of Age and Race." Washington, DC: U.S. Government Printing Office.

Lincoln, C. Eric.1973. *The Black Muslims in America*. Boston, MA: Beacon Press.

Litoff, Judy Barrett. 1978. *American Midwives: 1860 to the Present*. Westport, CT: Greenwood Press.

Logan, Rayford W. 1965. *The Betrayal of the Negro: From Rutherford B. Hayes to Woodrow Wilson*. London: Collier Books.

Lomax, Walter P. 1994."Medicaid Managed Care in Pennsylvania: The HMA Experience." *J.N.M.A.* 86 (6): 423.

Lyons, Babara, Diane Rowland and Kristina Manson. "Another Look at Medicaid." *Generations: Journal of the American Society on Aging* 20 (2): 24–30.

Mason, Philip. 1970. *Patterns of Dominance*. New York: Oxford University Press.

Massey, Douglas S. and Nancy A. Denton. 1993. *American Apartheid*. Cambridge, MA: Harvard University Press.

Maynard, Aubre de L. 1985 *A Gallery of Negro Surgeons*. (volumes 1 and 2, n.p., n.d.) . The Amistad Research Center, New Orleans, Louisiana, 21–23 November.

McHollin, Mattie and Cheryl Hamburg. 1991. "Black Medical Education in Tennessee." Fall Meeting of Tennessee Archivists. 15 November. Unpublished ms.

Memmi, Albert. 1967. *The Colonizer and The Colonized*. Boston: Beacon Press.

Message from the Director. 1986. "The Malpractice Crisis: Its Impact on the Elderly." Update-Newsletter, Center for Aging, University of Alabama at Birmingham 5 (3): 1–6.

Montgomery, James Riley. 1966. The Volunteer State Forges Its University: The University of Tennessee, 1887–1919. *The University of Tennessee Record* 69 (6):131–145.

Morantz, Regina Markell, Cynthia Stodola Pomerleau, and Carol Hansen Fenichel, eds. *In Her Own Words: Oral Histories of Women Physicians*. New Haven, CT: Yale University.

Morgan, Randall C. 1996. "Ethical Issues in Managed Care." *J.N.M.A.* 88 (8): 479–480.

Morias, Rudolph. 1978. *African American Physicians*. New York: Basic, p. 30.

Myrdal, Gunnar. 1996. *An American Dilemma: The Negro Problem and Modern Democracy*. New Brunswick, NJ: Transaction Publishers.

National Data Book. 1992. *Statistical Abstract of the United States 1992*. Washington, DC: U.S. Department Commerce, Economics and Statistics Administration, Bureau of the Census.

Norman, John C., ed. 1969. *Medicine in the Ghetto*. New York: Appleton-Century Crofts.

Oakleaf, Zoe D. 1984."Ozark Mountain and European White Witches," pp. 71–86 in Wilbur H. Watson (ed.), *Black Folk Medicine: The Therapeutic Significances of Faith and Trust*. New Brunswick, NJ: Transaction Publishers.

Organ, Claude H., Jr. and Margaret M. Kosiba, eds. 1987. *A Century of Black Surgeons: The U.S.A. Experiences*, vols. 1 and 2. Norman, OK: Transcript Press.

Overall, J.E. 1916. *The Story of Tennessee*. Dansville, NY: F.A. Owen Publishing Company.

Parsons, Talcott. 1951. *The Social System*. New York: The Free Press.

———. 1951."Social Structure and Dynamic Process: The Case of Modern Medical Practice," pp. 428–479 in *The Social System*, by Talcott Parsons. New York: The Free Press.

Pinkney, Alphonso. 1984. *The Myth of Black Progress*. New York: Cambridge University Press.

Platt, Samuel Joseph and Mary Louise Ogden. 1969. *Medical Men and Institutions of Knox County Tennessee*, 1789–1957. Knoxville, TN: S.B. Newman Printing Company.

Rivo, Marc L. and David A. Kindig. 1996."A Report Card on the Physician Work Force in the United States." *The New England Journal of Medicine* 334 (14): 892–896.

Rix, Sara E. and Tania Romashko. 1980. *With a Little Help From My Friends*. Washington, DC: American Institutes for Research.

Roback, Gene, Lillian Randolph, Bradley Seidman and Thomas Pasko. 1994. Physician Characteristics and Distribution in the United States. Washington, D.C.: American Medical Association, Department of Data Services.

Roman, Charles Victor. 1934. *History of Meharry Medical College*. Nashville, TN: Sunday School Publishing Board, The National Baptist Convention, Inc.

Rose, Arnold. 1948. *The Negro American,* with a foreword by Gunnar Myrdal. Boston: The Beacon Press.

Sammons, Vivian Overton. 1990. *Blacks in Science and Medicine*. New York: Hemmisphere Publishing Corporation.

Savitt, Todd L. 1978. *Medicine and Slavery: The Diseases and Health Care of Blacks in Antebellum Virginia*. Urbana, IL: University of Illinois Press.

Schwartz, George E. 1971."Educational Characteristics of Members of the National Medical Association." *Journal of Medical Education* 46 (July): 599.

Scott, Veronica J. 1988. "Major Physical Disorders among Older Rural Blacks," pp. 1–10 in Wilbur H. Watson (ed.), *Epidemiolgy of Life Threatening Disorders among Older Blacks*. Atlanta, GA: Atlanta University Center on Health and Aging.

Selden, Dana J. "Health Care Ethics," pp. 468–537 in Anthony R. Kovner, *Jona's Health Care Delivery* (see especially the discussion of "The Two Tier System of Health Care," p. 503).

Slater, Jack. 1972."Condemned to Die for Science." *Ebony* 28 (1): 177–193.

Snow, Loudell F. 1974. "Folk Medical Beliefs and Their Implications for Care of Patients: A Review Based on Studies Among Black Americans." *Annals of Internal Medicine* 81: 82–96.

Soderlund, Jean R. 1985. *Quakers and Slavery: A Divided Spirit*. Princeton, NJ: Princeton University Press.

Sollors, Werner; Thomas A. Underwood and Caldwell Titcomb, eds. 1986. *Varieties of Black Experience at Harvard: An Anthology*. Cambridge, MA: Harvard University Department of African-American Studies.

Stanfield, John. 1987. "Epilogue," pp. –227234 in Charles S. Johnson, *Bitter Canaan: The Story of The Negro Republic*. New Brunswick, NJ: Transaction Publishers.

Starr, Paul. 1982. *The Social Transformation of American Medicine*. New York: Basic Books.

Statistical Abstract of the United States. 1996. The National Data Book. U.S. Department of Commerce, Economics and Statistical Administration, Bureau of the Census, October.

Sterling, Dorothy, ed. 1984. *We Are Your Sisters: Black Women in the Nineteenth Century*. New York: W.W. Norton and Company.

Sterling, Rosalyn P. 1987. "Female Surgeons: The Dawn of a New Era," pp. 587–588 in Claude H. Organ, Jr. and Margaret M. Kosiba (eds.) *A Century of Black Surgeons: The U.S.A. Experience*, vol. II. Norman, OK: Transcript Press.

Stern, Bernard J. 1959. *Historical Sociology: The Selected Papers of Bernard J. Stern*. New York: The Citadel Press.

Summerville, James. 1983. *Educating Black Doctors: A History of Meharry Medical College*. Tuscaloosa, AL: The University of Alabama Press.

Twaddle, Andrew C. and Richard M. Hessler. 1977. *A Sociology of Health*. St. Louis, MO: C.V. Mosby.

Twumasi, Patrick A. 1975. *Medical Systems in Ghana: A Study in Medical Sociology*. Accra-Tema, Ghana: Ghana Publishing Corporation.

Van den Berghe, Pierre L. 1967. *Race and Racism: A Comparative Perspective*. New York: John Wiley and Sons.

Veal, Yvonne Smith. 1995."Wanted: A Few Committed African-American Physicians." *J.N.M.A.* 87 (8): 529–530.

Veterans Administration Medical Center. 1981. "In Observance of Black History Month, 1981." Tuskegee, AL: Veterans Administration Medical Center, February.

Walsh, Mary Roth. 1977. *Doctors Wanted, No Women Need Apply: Sexual Barriers in the Medical Profession, 1835–1975*. New Haven, CT: Yale University Press.

Waters, Donald J., ed. 1983. *Strange Ways and Sweet Dreams: Afro-American Folklore from the Hampton Institute*. Boston, MA: G.K. Hall and Company.

Watson, Wilbur H., ed. 1984. *Black Folk Medicine: The Therapeutic Significance of Faith Trust*. New Brunswick, NJ: Transaction Publishers.

———. 1972. *Body Idiom in Face to Face Interaction: A Field Study of Geriatric Nursing*. Philadelphia, PA: Van Pelt Library, University of Pennsylvania (unpublished Ph.D. diss.)

————. 1976. "Touching Behavior: Geriatric Nursing." *Journal of Communication* 25 (3):101–112.

Watson, Wilbur H. and Robert J. Maxwell. 1977.*Human Aging and Dying: A Study in Sociocultural Gerontology*. New York: St. Martins Press.

Watson, Wilbur H. 1982. *Aging and Social Behavior: An Introduction to Social Gerontology*. Belmont, CA: Wadsworth.

————. 1986. "Field Notes and Early Thoughts on Black Physicians and Separatism in the United States" Atlanta, GA: Atlanta University Center on Health and Aging.

————. 1989. *The Village: An Oral Historical and Ethnographic Study of a Black Community*. Atlanta, GA: Village Vanguard.

Wesley, Jr., Nathaniel. 1983. "Searching For Survival: Black Hospitals Listing and Selected Commentary." Washington, DC: Howard University School of Business Administration, January.

Welsing, Francis Cress. 1991. *The Isis Papers: The Keys to the Colors*. Chicago: Third World Press.

Wilkinson, Doris Y. 1992. "The 1850 Harvard Medical School Dispute and the Admission of African American Students." *Harvard Library Bulletin* 3 (3): 13–27.

Wilson, William J. 1987. *The Truly Disadvantaged. Chicago*. Chicago, IL: University of Chicago Press.

Wright, Charles H. 1995. *The National Medical Association Demands Equal Opportunity: Nothing More, Nothing Less*. Southfield, MI: Charro Book Company, 1995.

Young, James Clay. 1981.*Medical Choice in a Mexican Village*. New Brunswick, NJ: Rutgers University Press.

Index